# Changing Schools

Perspectives on five years
of education reform

Edited by Robert Peal

**A John Catt Publication**

## First Published 2015

by John Catt Educational Ltd,
12 Deben Mill Business Centre, Old Maltings Approach,
Melton, Woodbridge IP12 1BL

Tel: +44 (0) 1394 389850 Fax: +44 (0) 1394 386893
Email: enquiries@johncatt.com
Website: www.johncatt.com

## ISBN: 978 1 908095 30 5

Set and designed by John Catt Educational Limited

Printed and bound in Great Britain
by Charlesworth Press

# Contents

# Introduction

## Robert Peal

In 1993 David Green, now the Director of the think tank Civitas, wrote *Reinventing Civil Society*. Green argued for a revived sense of civic mission within public services, and on English schools he wrote, 'there can be no better example of how, if the state does too much, it narrows the scope for personal idealism and achievement.' Green went on to argue that new schools independent of local authority control should be allowed to form. He explained:

> A policy of de-regulation will allow new schools to be founded built around teacher commitment where it exists. This approach would be especially advantageous in inner-city areas because it would permit teachers with a special sense of mission to assist the poor by founding new schools.[1]

Twenty-two years on, this serves as a good description of what I currently see taking place within the profession.

As a full time history teacher, I feel fortunate to have entered a profession where the rolling back of the state's influence, and an emerging sense of *glasnost*, is unleashing a new wave of professional idealism. Gone are the days when the sense of ubiquity within English state schools was succinctly expressed by the phrase 'bog-standard comprehensive'. Instead, each holiday or half-term I meet teacher friends with exciting stories to tell about what they have seen at Michaela Community School, or at Dixons Trinity Academy, or at Reach Academy Feltham.

Reforms towards greater school autonomy, and the freedom to establish new independent state schools, have created a situation where more 'exemplar schools' can emerge, and make a radical contribution to the education debate.

Seeing a remarkable school in action has a power to alter one's views on education in a way that no graph, effect size or education conference discussion can equal. Due to recent reforms, the number of such exemplar schools is ever growing. Be it the GCSE results at King Solomon Academy, the Russell Group university entrances at the London Academy of Excellence, or the record breaking key stage 1 results at Ark Conway Primary School, exemplar schools are providing instructive models for the rest of the education sector to admire and emulate. As the achievements, and more importantly the methods, of such schools become better known, improvements should cascade through the sector.

Frequently, I have heard or read educators say that a visit to one school – Mossbourne Academy in Hackney – fundamentally changed their mind on an educational issue, most normally the potential to establish good behaviour with the intake of an inner-city comprehensive. In his book *Education, Education, Education* Andrew Adonis, the former Labour Minister for Schools and founder of the academies programme, testifies to the power of visiting such a school:

I regularly took or sent potential sponsors, and anyone else who needed persuading of the merits of academies, to visit Mossbourne. 'Let's not have this argument,' became my standard response to objections from MPs, councillors and defenders of the old comprehensive model. 'Just go and see an academy for yourself, and tell me what you think.' They usually came back saying they wanted one.[2]

It was Andrew Adonis who established the current movement towards greater school autonomy fifteen years ago, and the policy was supercharged by the coalition government from 2010. As David Cameron's former Director of Policy James O'Shaughnessy explains in Chapter 1, Michael Gove took the nascent Labour reform of City Academies, which had produced 204 state schools independent of local authority control, and rolled it out nationwide. Five years later, 60% of all English secondary schools and 14% of primary schools are academies – around 4,500 in total.

In addition, new academies known as 'free schools' can now be set up from scratch. This makes it possible for ambitious teachers to develop new entrants to the state school system, heralding an unprecedented opportunity for innovation. To see how one inspirational Headteacher is using her newfound freedoms, read Katherine Birbalsingh's account of her free school Michaela Community School in Chapter 2.

However, there is a paradox at the centre of these reforms, addressed by Jonathan Simons in his list of nine future policy challenges in Chapter 6. The coalition government simultaneously claimed to grant more autonomy and freedom to schools, whilst also driving up standards through centralised reforms. Could both claims have been true simultaneously?

Such a paradox can perhaps be understood when you split the government reforms into qualifications and curriculum, which has seen centralising reforms, and school administration, which has seen greater autonomy. In essence, the centralising measures of the coalition government were aimed at raising the academic bar, but the means by which schools meet this bar has become – to an unprecedented extent – down to them.

For an explanation of the government's reforms of qualifications and assessment, see Tina Isaacs's account in Chapter 3. Years of unchecked grade inflation, denied by schools and politicians alike, coupled with manipulation of controlled assessment, have come to an end. GCSE and A-level examinations are be reformed to become more challenging, and the perverse incentives created by performance measures such as 5 A$^*$ to C – which encouraged schools to focus their attentions overwhelmingly on pupils at the borderline between D and C grades – are being curtailed. The Ebacc, along with the upcoming 'Progress eight', are new accountability measures that instead encourage schools to focus on the achievement of all pupils across a broad range of academic subjects.

Aside from academisation, a range of smaller coalition reforms enhanced school autonomy. Schools no longer have to assess pupil work using National Curriculum Levels; schools can now train their own staff; schools can elect how to support disadvantaged pupils through the pupil premium; and classroom teachers can (if

Ofsted are to be believed) use whatever teaching methods they see fit. Illustrative of this greater freedom, between 2011 and 2012, the DfE guidance on 39 different areas ranging from Admissions to Youth Support was cut by three quarters, from 28,455 pages to just 6,978.[3]

These reforms reflect an awareness that a grass roots culture change, not a top down political change, is what is needed for English schools to improve. As the Schools Minister Nick Gibb concluded in a speech in November 2014, "good government does not improve public services. It enables public services to improve themselves."[4]

However, for such a culture change to take place, it must be driven by classroom teachers. In Chapter 7, Tom Bennett explains what will be needed for teaching to become a mature profession, profiling some encouraging developments such as the spread of Teach Meets and the growth of researchED.

In Chapter 4, Daisy Christodoulou reflects on how the end of National Curriculum levels grants teachers a new level of freedom in designing their own assessment systems. She explains some key principles of assessment that will allow them to do so effectively.

I am optimistic about the extent to which the teaching profession is rising to meet this challenge. In Chapter 5, the prominent teacher blogger Andrew Old explains how the coalition's education reforms have been criticised, supported, and in some cases influenced by the increasingly loud voice of frontline teachers communicating via social media – one of the most encouraging developments of the past five years.

He counts over 1273 active education blogs, and explains how they have provided the opportunity for teachers to dissent from the mainstream ideas of the education establishment. Blogs about pedagogy have challenged the professional orthodoxy in favour of child-centred teaching methods, whilst anonymous blogs have allowed front line teachers to lift the lid on what was *really* happening in our schools.

Where once groundless fads such as learning styles and Brain Gym were foisted upon the profession, teachers – led by Tom Bennett and the researchEd events – have become far more discerning judges of the evidence concerning how children learn. When one looks back at the fads that were endemic within schools up until a few years ago, such as learning styles, multiple intelligences and Brain Gym, along with the poor quality of research promoted by now defunct quangos such as the GTC, it his hard not to conclude significant progress has been made on this front.

These attacks on professional orthodoxies from the blogosphere have been accompanied by government reforms that have weakened the education establishment's monopoly over the education 'thoughtworld'. The expansion of school-based teacher training challenges the status of university education departments as the dominant providers of initial teacher training. Meanwhile, a minor 'bonfire of the quangos' has taken place, robbing many self-styled 'educationists' of the stage from which they previously pronounced their ideas. By his own count, Michael Gove scrapped nine education quangos, in addition to slimming down those that remained.

Wherever one stands on the debate over skills and knowledge, or child-centred and teacher-led instruction, it is encouraging that frontline teachers – at the expense of university academics and quangocrats – are finding an increasingly voice within such debates. I am delighted that half the contributors to this book are, or have until very recently been, full-time teachers in state schools.

In Chapter 8, the American school reformers Doug Lemov and Joaquin Hernandez imagine an argument between two school Heads: one a believer in a knowledge curriculum and direct instruction, the other an adherent to thinking skills and project-based learning. How should their debate be settled? As Lemov and Hernandez write, both should be allowed to pursue their separate ideas, and the argument should be settled by results alone. As they write, 'choice allows us to stop arguing and start implementing'. In England, we at long last have a schools system where this is becoming possible.

If the mark of a successful idea is that its critics go from outright opposition, to enthusiastic endorsement, without ever claiming that their mind has changed – then perhaps the arguments for greater school freedom is winning the day. Recently, *The Guardian* published a 'long read', in part profiling of one of our contributors Doug Lemov and his chain of American Charters, Uncommon Schools. The author stated:

> The rise of charter schools and academies has precipitated a Cambrian explosion of new ideas and innovations, stimulating a debate about methodology led by teachers themselves... After years of debate among academics and politicians over how to raise teacher standards, the problem is being solved by the practitioners.[5]

This, coming from a newspaper that ten years ago was publishing fortnightly satirical attacks on 'Kafka Academy', and which in 2004 claimed that the city academy programme 'sounds the death knell of the old comprehensive system', must show something like progress.[6]

Michael Gove was the fourth longest serving Education Secretary since 1945. Including his time from 2007 as Shadow Secretary of State for Education, Gove spent over seven years with the education brief. Overhearing conversations after Gove's speeches, I would often hear those opposed to his reforms nevertheless concede that his mastery of his brief was remarkable.

The enormous challenge of reforming British education was well testified to by Gove's predecessors. Kenneth Baker wrote in his memoirs that the Education Department had the 'strongest in-house ideology' of all Whitehall departments, whilst one of Kenneth Clarke's advisers remembered education reform as 'like walking in treacle.'[7] Memorably, George Walden recalled being told that reforming education as like 'trying to disperse a fog with a hand grenade: after the flash and the explosion, the fog creeps back.'[8]

Whether the 'fog' creeps back this time is yet to be seen. However, Gove's reforms may well be significant enough to be sustained by their own momentum. Schools now enjoy a level of autonomy that no future politician will be able to remove; classroom teachers are creating more rigorous school curriculums; and academisation has spawned powerful new players in the education game – namely highly successful academy chains such as Harris and Ark. Michael Gove's reforms, it could be argued, are only just beginning.

The great American reformer and Democrat Senator Daniel Patrick Moynihan once wrote that 'The central conservative truth is that it is culture, not politics, that determines the success of a society. The central liberal truth is that politics can change a culture and save it from itself.'[9] What is true of society at large is also true of schools. I am hopeful then recent political reforms have created the conditions in which English state schools are finally able to change their own cultures for the better.

## Endnotes

1   Green, D. (1993) *Reinventing Civil Society: The Rediscovery of Welfare Without Politics*, Institute of Economic Affairs, p. 115, 117.

2   Adonis, A. (2012) *Education, Education, Education: Reforming England's Schools*, Biteback, p. 6.

3   Department for Education, 'Briefing: DfE Guidance Reductions'.

4   Gibb, N. 'The Fruits of Autonomy', speech to Reform on 12 November 2014.

5   Leslie, I. 'The revolution that could change the way your child is taught', *The Guardian*, March 11 2015.

6   Smithers, R. 'Five year education plan: Comprehensive change drives Labour's agenda', *The Guardian*, July 9 2004.

7   Peal, R. (2014) *Progressively Worse: The Burden of Bad Ideas in British Schools*, Civitas, chapter 4.

8   Walden, G. 'Our education system condemns children to second-class lives', *Telegraph*, August 22 2009.

9   Moynihan, D. P. (1996) *Miles to Go: A Personal History of Social Policy*, Harvard University Press, p. 63.

# About the Contributors

**Robert Peal** is Head of History at the West London Free School, and an honorary research fellow at the think tank Civitas. Having trained as a history teacher through Teach First, he taught for two years in the West Midlands before joining Civitas. At Civitas, he wrote a book chronicling the history of progressive education from the 1960s to today entitled *Progressively Worse*, and a report on Ofsted inspections entitled *Playing the Game*.

**James O'Shaughnessey** is an education entrepreneur. He founded and runs Floreat Education, a family of primary schools that helps pupils flourish by cultivating their minds and developing their character virtues. James chairs the International Positive Education Network and is a co-founder of EDSPACE. Before working in education he was director of policy to the Prime Minister.

**Katharine Birbalsingh** is Headmistress of Michaela Community School in Brent. Born in Canada, she was educated at a Midlands Comprehensive and has a degree in Philosophy and Modern Languages from Oxford. Katharine has visited and taught in schools across the globe, including China, India, USA and South Africa. She has published in various newspapers and magazines and written two books. Her blog about everyday life in a London Comprehensive was turned into a book, *To Miss with Love*, in 2011.

**Dr Tina Isaacs** is a senior lecturer at the UCL Institute of Education. She is programme director for the MA in Educational Assessment and a director at the Institute's Centre for Post-14 Research and Innovation. Before joining the IOE she worked for 16 years at the National Council for Vocational Qualifications (NCVQ), the Qualifications and Curriculum Authority (QCA) and the Office of Qualifications and Examinations Regulation (Ofqual) specialising in 14–19 qualifications development, implementation, accreditation and monitoring.

**Daisy Christodoulou** is the Research and Development Manager at Ark Schools, where she works on new approaches to curriculum and assessment. Before that, she trained as a secondary English teacher through the Teach First programme and taught in two London comprehensives. Her book, *Seven Myths about Education*, was published in March 2014.

**Andrew Old** is a maths teacher in the West Midlands. He has been blogging on the 'Scenes From The Battleground' blog since 2006. He is also editor of the Labour Teachers blog and the Echo Chamber blog. He studied education policy as part of his masters degree in Education Leadership from the University of Warwick.

**Jonathan Simons** is the Head of Education at Policy Exchange. Previously, he worked at Serco Group where he was Director of Strategy and Market Development in both the company's specialist education and health practices. Prior to that, he was Head of Open Public Services in the Cabinet Office, and Head of Education in the Prime Minister's Strategy Unit. Jonathan is also the Chair of Governors and Co-Founder of Greenwich Free School.

**Tom Bennett** is a teacher in East London and a columnist for the *TES*. Since 2008 he has authored or co-authored six books on teacher training and professional development. In 2013 he founded researchED, a grass roots organisation designed to repair the relationship between practice and research in education. He is a member of an expert panel set up by the DfE to redesign the core offer in UK initial teacher training.

**Joaquin Hernandez** is a professional development content designer for the Teach Like a Champion Team at Uncommon Schools. In this role, he screens footage of classrooms, provides in-depth analysis of great teaching, and designs training for use inside and outside of Uncommon. Prior to this role, Joaquin worked as a high school history teacher in Washington, D.C. and was a Manager, Teacher Leadership Development for Teach For America.

**Doug Lemov** is a Managing Director at Uncommon Schools, which runs 42 high performing charter schools in under-served communities in the northeastern US. He is the author of *Teach Like a Champion 2.0* and *Practice Perfect*.

# Academies and chains: When competition meets collaboration

## James O'Shaughnessy

Politicians might not like to admit it, but the path of education reform over the last forty years has actually been rather bi-partisan. Some of the ideas that first appeared in Labour Prime Minister James Callaghan's 'secret garden' speech in 1976 – a central curriculum, national standards, a beefed-up inspectorate – have been at the heart of successive governments' policy frameworks. Yet the one proposal that, arguably, has dominated education debate over the last 15 years – school autonomy – seems to stand in contrast to Callaghan's argument that the state should exercise more control and oversight over schools.

How did we reach the point where the so-called standards movement, formed both here and in the US to fight against the regressive effects of misguided teaching ideologies, came to favour institutional freedom over central prescription? And how did the growth of academies and free schools (independently run but state-funded schools) come to dominate the agenda of a Conservative Party that had hitherto preferred to prescribe how schools should improve behaviour and make teaching more rigorous?

### The academies programme

In the post war period, all state-funded schools have tended to be either controlled by the local authority (known as maintained schools) or by the churches (known as voluntary-controlled or voluntary-aided schools). The first significant break with this pattern was the creation of 15 City Technology Colleges (CTCs) following the 1988 Education Reform Act. These schools were owned and run by charities set up by a range of organisations, from philanthropists (The Harris CTC) to industry bodies (the BRIT School) to livery companies (Haberdashers' Aske's Hatcham College).

These new schools occupied a new niche in the state sector: they were regular state-funded schools, open to all, but with a range of operational freedoms and the benefit of a sponsor who could provide funds or other resources to support the success of the school. The CTCs were quickly followed by grant-maintained (GM) status, a radical new mechanism that allowed schools to leave local authority control, which was taken up by over a thousand schools between 1988 and 1998. Both CTCs and GM schools set the template for the later academies.

The seeds of the school autonomy movement were thus sown in the last Conservative government, and had their roots in a desire to give schools the freedom to breath outside of local authority control. While the 1988 Act was undoubtedly a centralising piece of legislation, introducing both the National Curriculum and Ofsted, it was also inspired by a desire to take local authorities out of the business of running schools:

especially those authorities addicted to the progressive teaching ideologies that were wreaking havoc with literacy and numeracy standards. Since then there has been a ongoing conflict between centralising tendencies in the name of standards and liberalising policies in the name of freedom and innovation, something that has been a defining feature of the coalition government.

Showing that the bi-partisan path of reform is not always smooth, one of the first actions of the incoming Blair government was to remove the freedoms from the GM schools through its 1998 Act. And yet the CTCs remained, eventually providing inspiration for the head of the No.10 Policy Unit Andrew Adonis, now Lord Adonis, as he sought for solutions to deal with deeply ingrained failure in what he estimated to be the 5% of secondary schools producing truly disastrous results for their pupils.[1]

As Adonis sets out in his memoir of the period, he arrived at the proposal for academies – charitable schools operating in the state sector, with freedoms on who to employ and what to teach – by coming across the impact the 15 CTCs were having on standards in areas where educational performance had previously been very low. He realised that the injection of energy, time and, critically, money from a sponsor could break the cycle of underachievement, raise expectations and begin to rescue the hundreds of thousands of pupils whose lives were being wrecked by failing schools. Adonis realised that all the centralising policies in the world could not bring about the dramatic culture change need to transform these schools, and only their total rebuilding and reimagining could hope to do so. The City Academies programme was born.

Between 2000 and 2010, Adonis, first as an adviser and then as minister, helped bring about the creation of 204 academies in the face of extraordinary opposition from vested interests such as local authorities, teaching unions, campaign groups like the Local Schools Network, and the education department itself. Critical to the success of the programme was support from successive Prime Ministers, Tony Blair and Gordon Brown, and the broad political spectrum of the sponsors involved. The two other main parties came on board with the programme, with the Conservatives – sensing the legacy of their previous CTC and GM programmes – especially positive.

That support was transformed into full-throated evangelism with the appointment of Michael Gove as Shadow Education Secretary in 2007. Gove had been Chairman of the think tank Policy Exchange when it was doing a great deal of research on how to transform schools standards. His enthusiasm for spreading school autonomy beyond the City Academies was influenced by a paper written in 2005 by Charlotte Leslie and me, *More Good School Places*, calling for all good schools to be given the chance to gain the autonomy experienced by academies.[2] By the end of 2007 this became the official position of the Conservative Party, and plans were hatched to allow schools to convert to academy status under a Conservative government.

Michael Gove became a zealous advocate of the importance of school autonomy, both for existing schools and for what, in the 2007 policy green paper *Raising the Bar, Closing the Gap*, were known as new academies, but which we now call free schools.[3]

Work began on draft legislation that could be introduced to allow for three new types of academies. Following the 2010 election and his elevation to Prime Minister, the first legislative act of David Cameron's government was the Academies Act 2010. This created:

- *converter academies*: schools rated good or outstanding could transfer out of local authority control. Essentially a retread of the GM system.

- *sponsored academies*: underperforming schools, rated inadequate by Ofsted, would be taken over and rebooted by sponsors. A continuation of the original Labour government's City Academy programme.

- *free schools (new academies)*: brand new schools in areas of need or poor standards. The CTC programme with rocket boosters.

Since the coalition reforms the pace of change has accelerated rapidly. By the end of the Parliament, the number of academies was over 4,500, with a further 270 applications in process. Added to the circa 400 free schools open or in pre-opening, this means that over 25% of the total school estate now enjoys academy status, although the numbers within that are heavily skewed: only 14% of primary schools are academies of one form or another, whereas the figure is 60% for secondary.[4]

## Academies: a technical definition

Academies occupy a separate legal status to government maintained schools. In fact, each 'qualifying academy proprietor', *ie* academy trust, is established as a Company Limited by Guarantee, whose object is a charitable purpose for advancing education [Academies Act 2010]. In this regard, academies must comply with company law as set out in the Companies Act 1985 and the requirements of the Charity Commission, especially in regard to the Charities' Statement of Recommended Practice (SORP). These legal requirements are principally related to financial management, meaning that academies must produce their accounts, in a prescribed format, and that they must be independently audited by a registered auditor.

While they are constituted as charities, academies are exempt from having to register with the Charity Commission and are principally regulated by the Education Funding Agency on behalf of the Department for Education (DfE). Any educational endowment or academic fund established under the academy company is also exempt from registration.

The academy trust enters into a funding agreement with the Secretary of State for the running of the academy, with both parties signing Articles of Association outlining the constitution of the school. From this point the academy trust takes strategic responsibility for the running of the academy, entering into contracts (such as school improvement services), and ownership of land and other assets. The trust appoints the governors (also known as directors or trustees) to manage the academy on its behalf.

## The history of school autonomy

Academies and academy chains are a current manifestation of a much older phenomenon within our education system.[5] Independent groupings of schools have been a feature of our school system for hundreds of years. Such groupings have long provided opportunities for economies of scale, dispersal of pedagogical practice, and peer-to-peer collaboration, and today offer the most sustainable route towards a continually improving school system. It is my view that the period of municipalised control of schools in the twentieth century, which began in earnest with the 1902 Education Act and became dominant after the Second World War, is the historical aberration, not the other way round.

The Forster Act of 1870 attempted to protect private, charitable and religious control of schools, thereby guaranteeing plurality and autonomy, while using state funds to ensure coverage, quality and access through establishment of school boards where voluntary efforts were not enough. This Act set up the dual-system: local school boards providing non-denominational schools on the rates, and religious and other foundations providing schools funded by endowments and government grants. One of the effects of the introduction of school boards was a huge surge in the creation of voluntary schools – between 1870 and 1876 1.5 million school places were created but only a third by school boards.[6]

School federations or groups have been around for centuries. The King Edward School Foundation in Birmingham, which dates from the 16th Century and in 2010 sponsored its first academy conversion, is arguably the oldest non-religious school group in England. Many schools are already in harder or softer partnerships with other schools, crossing state and independent sectors. The City Livery companies have provided secondary education for centuries. The mid-19th century saw the creation of the Church Schools Company in 1883 (now the United Church Schools Trust, which through its sister charity the United Learning Trust is one of England's biggest academy chains) and the creation of Woodard Schools from 1849 onwards, which is now an academy sponsor. The Endowed Schools Act of 1869 opened up school endowments to the use of girls, with separate schools for boys and girls arising out of the same foundations. It also provoked the creation of the Women's Educational Union to support a new 'Public Day School for Girls' – the origin of the Girls Day School Trust, also now an academy sponsor as well as deliverer of independent schooling.

The move back towards school autonomy and a more collaborative, pluralist supply of education embodied in the emergence of academy chains should be seen as a reversion to the historical norm. Indeed, to understand the power, relevance and durability of chains one only needs to look at the sponsors of the original wave of academy schools that opened in the first five years of the scheme between 2002 and 2006. As well as seeing the beginnings of some of the now very well-known chains, such as the Harris Federation and Ark, there were also at least nine existing organisations with historical involvement in the delivery of education to one degree or another:

1. The Diocese of London (Greig City Academy)
2. The United Learning Trust, a sister trust to the United Church
3. Schools Trust (Manchester Academy, The King's Academy, Lambeth Academy,
4. Northampton Academy, Trinity Academy and Salford City Academy)
5. City of London Corporation (City of London Academy)
6. The Mercers' Company (Walsall Academy)
7. The Roman Catholic Archdiocese of Southwark (St Paul's Academy)
8. Haberdashers' Livery Company (Haberdashers' Aske's Knights Academy,
9. Haberdashers' Aske's Hatcham College)
10. Diocese of Liverpool and the Roman Catholic Archdiocese of Liverpool (The
11. Academy of St Francis of Assisi) Diocese of Ripon and Leeds (David Young Community Academy)
12. CFBT Education Trust (St Mark's Church of England Academy).

This is fairly remarkable given how hostile the operating environment was for these kinds of organisations in the heavily local-authority dominated post-war era. And as the academy programme has developed so more and more charitable educational trusts, both existing and emergent, have become involved.

## What works?

In addition to the historical strength of England's independently run schools, the move back towards school autonomy was driven by a range of other factors. As Tony Blair once said, "what matters is what works", a maxim implicit in the comments of the Chief Inspector of Schools, Sir Michael Wilshaw, in a speech to Policy Exchange on 20 March 2012. He said there was now a "growing consensus across the major parties that the principle of school autonomy, matched with accountability, works. Indeed, the recent evidence from Professor Michael Barber on successful jurisdictions which operate according to this principle is incontrovertible".[7]

There is compelling and extensive evidence on the effectiveness of school autonomy in raising pupil outcomes, well summarised in the DfE's Academies Annual Report 2010/11: The Organisation for Economic Cooperation and Development (OECD) has stated: 'the creation of more autonomous schools will lead to innovations in curriculum, instruction and governance, which in turn will improve outcomes.'[8] Wößmann and Fuchs found that 'test scores are higher when schools manage their own budgets and recruit and select their own teachers.'[9] Hindriks *et al* examined the Flemish education system in Belgium and concluded that: 'We find strong indications that operational school autonomy is associated with high educational performance if appropriate accountability systems are active.'[10] Hanushek *et al* analysed PISA data and concluded: 'autonomy reforms improve student achievement in developed countries.'[11] Despite the hyperbole of many on the left – *The Guardian* actually ran the following news headline in 2012: 'Education system could be completely privatised by

2015, union predicts"[12] – what is actually happening is that the state schooling system is being turned into a classic public sector market. Consumers (parents and students) are given a choice, providers are encouraged to diversify and innovate, and new entrants are allowed into the market. However, prices are fixed at the level the state is prepared to pay, the publication of performance data is required and there are strict regulations on how schools behave.

Many other countries have successfully trodden this path in education. They include countries as diverse as the USA, Hong Kong, Sweden and New Zealand. The reason they have done so, and that England (if not the rest of the UK) has followed, is that this kind of system provides the right conditions for schools to flourish. They enable and encourage collaboration between schools – in England this is done through multi-academy trusts, umbrella trusts, teaching schools alliances, initial teacher training programmes and so on – while also allowing competition between schools, which keeps practitioners focused on outcomes.

One of the defining features of the academy movement has been the emergence of a new form of organisation – academy chains. These are groups of institutions that are bound together legally, financially and operationally. The DfE estimates that there are around 500 chains in England, although the majority have fewer than five member schools. Usually they have formed in order to spread the benefits of a particular approach to teaching and school administration that has proven to be successful, as well as bringing other benefits such as the ability to drive out economies of scale.

Encouragingly, there is a growing body of evidence showing that school chains are more effective at improving results than single academies. Where the CTC, GM and City Academy programme typically saw schools becoming autonomous as single, standalone entities, this latest phase of reform has encouraged collaboration and formal links between schools. According to the Regional Schools Commissioner Dominic Herrington, in South London and the South East 47% of primary academies are in chains of between two and nine schools, as are 21% of secondaries.[13]

The purposeful mixture of collaboration and competition might seem paradoxical for some, but only if through a wilful misunderstanding of the way markets really work. Far from being the atomised, dog-eat-dog picture still painted by some on the left, real markets encourage innovation through collaboration *within* firms while all the time being kept consumer-focused by competition *between* firms. This idea even has a name – co-opetition – and is the subject of a book of that title by Harvard and Yale academics Adam Brandenburger and Barry Nalebuff.[14] Its application in education has been neatly described by former Head of the National College of School Leadership, Steve Munby, who said:

> So of course there is competition between schools and between organisations. We would not be strong leaders if that competitive edge wasn't there in us. We sometimes try to hide it and it is not fashionable to admit it in many quarters but it is there – let's not pretend otherwise. Competition stops us from being complacent

and keeps us on our toes. In fact, losing our competitive edge is a dangerous thing for leaders.

But, in my view, without collaboration our education system has no hope of being successful. If we have schools competing and not collaborating what we will get is greater variation in quality. Some will get better and do really well, but overall the system will not improve. The same can increasingly be said for multi-academy trusts.

But just as I believe competition for the sake of competition is unhelpful, so too is collaboration for the sake of getting along – the worst kind of collaboration is the sort that sees schools huddling together, endorsing each other's views and practices and generally keeping one another comfortable.[15]

## Are academies using their freedoms?

One of the concerns about the current programme is whether academies are really using the freedoms available to them to innovate and improve. In 2012 the think tank Reform and The Schools Network surveyed a range of academy leaders and found that the financial incentive of converting – extra funding that used to go to the local authority for the provision of services was instead routed straight to schools – was the most quoted reason for moving to academy status. Only 57% of schools wanted the opportunity to innovate to raise standards, while half (51%) wanted less local authority involvement in their school.[16] In 2012, law firm Browne Jacobson carried out a similar survey of primary and secondary Headteachers of converter academies and found a more positive picture about how these schools were taking advantage of their freedoms. Half of all recently converted academy schools had already used their freedoms to make changes to the way their school curriculum is delivered and another 20% expected to make changes within the next 12 months, even though only 5% of Headteachers identified it as the most important reason to become an academy.

The same research also found that, even for academies that were not taking advantage of their freedoms, just being out of local authority control was important. One third of schools stated that freedom from local authority control was their most important reason for becoming an academy, and of those interviewed nine out of ten have already exercised this freedom.[17]

This chimes with interviews I carried out for my 2012 Policy Exchange report *Competition meets Collaboration*. There is simply no desire among secondary Heads for local authorities to get involved once more in the delivery of education, although the picture for primaries is more nuanced. Even critics of government policy among the academy leaders feel that local authorities were often poor providers of education services such as curriculum development or professional development, and that the move away from council-as-provider was necessary on the grounds that most, though not all, had failed to adapt to the demands of the choice agenda. Besides, the dramatic cuts experienced by local authorities over the last five years have shrunk councils' ability to provide more than the most basic education services, and many authorities have instructed their schools to become academies and join chains so that they have a support network.

## Success so far

It is early days for both converter academies and free schools (new academies) and so hard to draw conclusions. Only in 2016, five years after they opened, will the initial wave of secondary free schools actually chalk up their first set of GCSE results. The current evidence on their effectiveness is mixed: the Education Select Committee failed to find strong evidence of the impact of converters on attainment, although the New Schools Network has pointed out that free schools are more likely than other schools to gain outstanding ratings from Ofsted.

While it is too early to know whether the converter academy programme has been successful, there is no ambiguity about the success of the original sponsored academies. The National Audit Office has looked at the performance of academies compared to a selected group of maintained schools and found a significant improvement in the proportion of pupils achieving the equivalent of five or more GCSEs at A*–C grade in the academies compared to the comparison group. Machin and Venoit for the London School of Economics looked at the performance of these schools:

> Our results suggest that moving to a more autonomous school structure through academy conversion generates a significant improvement in the quality of pupil intake, a significant improvement in pupil performance and small significant improvements in the performance of pupils enrolled in neighbouring schools. These results are strongest for the schools that have been academies for longer and for those who experience the largest increase in their school autonomy.

> These findings matter from an economic perspective, in that they suggest the increased autonomy and flexible governance enabled by academy conversion may have had the scope to sharpen incentives to improve performance. They also matter from a public policy standpoint because recent years have seen the increased prevalence of an education system that is being allowed to become more and more autonomous. In essence, the results paint a (relatively) positive picture of the academy schools that were introduced by the Labour government of 1997–2010. The caveat is that such benefits have, at least for the schools we consider, taken a while to materialise."[18]

DfE analysis has shown that, between 2005/06 and 2010/11, results for pupils in sponsored academies improved by 27.7 percentage points – a faster rate than in other state-funded schools (14.2 percentage points) and a faster rate than in a group of similar schools (21.3 percentage points).[19]

## The future: academy chains

If it is too soon to judge the impact of the most recent forms of academies (converter and free schools), is there anything useful we can say about groups of schools? We already know that such groups of schools have been a feature of our education system for decades, if not centuries, but their newest incarnation – academy chains – have only emerged in the last ten years.

On the upside, analysis by both Chapman *et al* and Hill *et al* for the National College found tentative evidence that academy and other federations outperformed single academies.[20] And research carried out for my 2012 Policy Exchange report found early evidence that chains of academies out-perform single academies, but with diminishing returns. The DfE's most recent statistical analysis does little to clarify the issue, with some chains clearly performing well and others seemingly acting as a drag anchor on their schools' performance.[21]

The commentary accompanying the DfE Working Paper asks readers for caution in how the results from the research are interpreted, but whatever the absolute numbers there are clear relative differences in performance from one chain to the next. The highest performers are familiar names – those frequently spoken of by politicians whenever they want to argue for the benefits of chains. In the cases of Ark and Harris, they have also benefited from the most significant injection of philanthropic donations of any of the chains. What, if anything, can we learn form this table other than more money might lead to better results?

Across two reports for the National College, consultant and former education special adviser Robert Hill found a series of advantages that could accrue from schools forming together into chains:

- Clear vision and values, describing the central driving educational ethos of the chain
- A distinct teaching and learning model
- A system for training leaders and other staff
- Deployment of key leaders across the chain
- Direct employment of all or key staff
- Geographical proximity
- Central resources and system
- Strong quality assurance arrangements
- Effective and clear governance

Furthermore, when interviewed by Hill, a series of advantages of expanding academy chains were identified by three-quarters of CEOs of sponsored academy chains:

- Extending the chain's impact in terms of raising standards of education for more young people
- Creating a broader base for developing leaders
- Increasing the scope for sharing learning, subject specialisms, school improvement expertise and CPD
- Providing more opportunities for staff deployment and promotion within the chain

- Increasing economies of scale in the running of central services and provides greater purchasing power
- Opening up new opportunities to build new primary/secondary curriculum and transition models
- Enabling central costs to be shared across a larger number of schools
- Providing a bigger platform for supporting innovation
- Providing a stronger brand to attract parents and applications for admission

My personal experience of studying chains, and visiting their schools and HQs, backs up Hill's observations. Ark and Harris are so successful because they display almost all of the above characteristics. The reason they do so is undoubtedly derived from the fact they have more resources than most, but it is much more than that. They have a clear central vision, a no-excuses culture, and a total focus on high academic standards and the factors that contribute to them like behaviour and staff training. The academy chains that appear to be struggling tend to be those that see their role as providing administrative support, with little in the way of distinct teaching and learning models or organisational visions and values. The best chains have good levels of capacity at the centre of the trust, a fairly top-down *modus operandi* which only grants schools within the chain autonomy once they have been bootstrapped and are good or better, and very strong leadership from both the CEO and the Trustees.

This pattern of behaviours is found in other successful groups of schools, like the KIPP charter schools in the US or in successful international groups of schools like those run by Cognita. It was what I am trying to instil in my own nascent primary school chain, Floreat Education. We have a clear and explicit mission, which is to develop pupils' character virtues and deliver a knowledge-rich academic curriculum, and are able to invest in the core team thanks to our fundraising efforts. Central to our approach is that pupils will not flourish unless teachers do, and so we are developing a sector-leader training and development programme called *Teacher Flourishing*. We are creating our own *Virtue and Knowledge School Model*, so that all our staff have the curricula, assessment and other tools they need to achieve our ambitious goals. On the corporate side, we intend to grow organically until we reach around 20-25 schools, all clustered within an hour's drive of one another in and around West London, where our first schools are opening this September. But it will take years to establish whether our plans to create the best primary schools in the country will actually come to fruition.

## Proposals for the future

When I went into government in 2010 as Director of Policy in No.10 it was my ambition that, if the coalition only managed a single term, then by the end of it the academy reform programme would be so embedded that it could not be reversed. As a long-time proponent of school autonomy that moment is tantalisingly close, but not yet achieved. A future, more hostile, government could still unwind much of the reform, although given the fiscal circumstances it is hard to foresee how it could afford to re-establish local authorities as the primary providers of state schooling. Besides, I am an optimist and believe that the next five years will bring about a much more autonomous school system, to the benefit of children, teachers, parents and school leaders alike.

Within that system, the most important institutional innovation has been the creation of academy chains. Their invention was never an object of policy, but history, theory, international practice and an emerging evidence base speak to their benefits. Ultimately, these groups of schools are effective by providing economies of scale and opportunities for frequent and productive peer-to-peer collaboration, the wellspring of innovation. Chains provide administrative support for each individual school, a task that frees up time for principals and teachers to focus on teaching. They act as 'internal auditors' in order to provide quality assurance and spread best practice, particularly as a way of improving professional development

What is exciting about the development of school chains is that it reflects the creation of a better-functioning public sector market where collaboration and competition both feature. The most important outcome of the supply-side reform movement (the main strands of which are autonomy and freedom to provide) has been the creation of school chains that deliver higher standards than standalone providers. But the reform is not yet completed. To reach that point, policy for the next five years should include getting all schools to transition to academy status, even if that is within trusts led by high-performing local authorities. To oil the wheel, the DfE should beef up its School Chain Growth Fund and provide a range of financial support to help schools join up into multi-school groups. Smaller successful chains should be capitalised by the Department – or another investor, if the politics can be made to work – to continue their growth towards a sustainable size.

All groups of schools will need to be regulated as groups, not just as individual schools, and that means being inspected directly by Ofsted or whatever may replace it. Chains that are failing needs to be broken up in an orderly way and schools given the freedom to choose a better group. To manage that element of the market the local or regional commissioners for school standards need to be given oversight for all schools, not just autonomous ones. That way the school system can move speedily to a thriving, dynamic market where parents have a range of choice and education providers are both collaborating and competing to be the best that they can be.

### Endnotes

1    Adonis, A. (2012) *Education, Education, Education: Reforming England's Schools*, Biteback Publishing.

2    O'Shaughnessy, J. and Leslie, C. (2005) *More Good School Places*, Policy Exchange.

3    Conservative Party (2007), *Raising the Bar, Closing the gap*, Policy Green Paper no. 1.

4    DfE, Open Academies Data, www.gov.uk/government/publications/open-academies-and-academy-projects-in-development [accessed April, 2015].

5   For a more detailed account, see O'Shaughnessy, J. (2012) *Competition Meets Collaboration: Helping school chains address England's long tail of educational failure*, Policy Exchange.

6   Barnard, H. C. (1961) *A History of English Education from 1760*, Hodder and Staughton.

7   Wilshaw, M. 'Not good enough: how should the system respond when schools need support?', speech to Policy Exchange on 20 March 2012.

8   OECD (2010), *Education at a Glance 2010: OECD Indicators*.

9   Wößmann, L. and Fuchs, T. (2004) *What Accounts for International Differences in Student Performance? A Re-examination Using PISA Data*, Working Paper no 1235, Germany.

10  Hindriks, J. *et al*, (2010) *School Autonomy and Educational Performance: Within-Country Evidence*, Centre for Operations Research and Econometrics, Discussion Paper no. 82, Belgium.

11  Hanushek, E. A. *et al*, (2011) *Does School Autonomy Make Sense Everywhere? Panel Estimates from PISA*, Discussion Paper no. 6185, IZA: Institute for the Study of Labor, Germany.

12  'Education system could be completely privatised by 2015, union predicts', *The Guardian*, 28 March 2012.

13  Regional Schools Commissioner for the South East and South London, *Newsletter: Issue 6*, 27 March 2015.

14  Brandenburger, A. M. and Nalebuff, B. J. (1997) *Co-Opetition*, Currency Doubleday.

15  Munby, S., speech to the *Sunday Times* Festival of Education at Wellington College on 21 June 2013 www.cfbt.com/en-GB/Useful-Links/sunday-times-festival-of-education-june-2013 [accessed April 2015]

16  Bassett, D. *et al*, (2012) *Plan A+ Unleashing the potential of academies*, The Schools Network and Reform.

17  Browne Jacobson (2012) *Academies – driving success through autonomy*.

18  Machin, S. and Vernoit, J. (2011) *Changing School Autonomy: Academy Schools and their Introduction to England's Education*, Centre for the Economic of Education, London School of Economics.

19  Gove, M. 'How are the Children? Achievement for all in the 21st Century', speech to the Spectator Education Conference, 26 June 2012.

20  Chapman, C. *et al*, (2011) *A study of the impact of school federation on student outcomes*, National College for School Leadership.

21  Department for Education (2015), *Statistical Working Paper: Measuring the performance of schools within academy chains and local authorities*.

# Free schools:
# Making success sustainable

## Katharine Birbalsingh

Recently I was at a teacher event behind a stall advertising our school, Michaela Community School, to potential staff recruits. The NUT's stall was opposite ours. When I first saw them there, I figured we had been given this particular stall as some sort of punishment. Members of the NUT have campaigned tirelessly to have our school closed down. First they tried to stop us from opening, and three years later, when we finally won that battle, they still regularly protest outside our school handing out leaflets to our Year 7 pupils, claiming that our building is a health and safety hazard. They once whipped up enough of a frenzy to get BBC cameras along; it came to nothing when the BBC realised there was no story.

So it was funny when the NUT representatives read our posters listing the reasons why teachers might want to work for us and declared that they loved our ethos. "It really fits with what we believe schools should be doing," said one NUT rep. "And I see you are a community school!"

"Erm, no... not exactly," I said sheepishly, "that's just our name... We're actually a free school." Silence. I was the enemy. I smiled. "Imagine that! We're a free school and we have an ethos that you approve of! Doesn't that make you question your belief that free schools should be closed down?"

In 2010, free schools, based on the well-established charter schools in America, became a reality in Britain. It took us three years to set up Michaela in part because our detractors fought a good fight. But here we are. And we are here to stay.

Michaela is all about its staff. If you take care of your staff, the pupils will take care of themselves. Or at least, the staff will take good care of the pupils, and that, after all, is what one really wants as a Head. At Michaela, the Senior Team (ST) is there to support the teachers, and we make decisions with their welfare at the heart of everything we do.

Our school has been open in Wembley Park, Brent, since September 2014. Things are going well now, but who knows what the future holds? All I can talk about here is what we are trying to achieve, the kind of school we hope to be one day. For the moment, we have 120 Year 7 pupils in classrooms off one corridor. One day, we'll have 840 pupils, including our sixth form. And I hope our attitude towards our staff remains the same. Michaela's view on staff has three elements to it:

1. Trust your staff to do a good job
2. Support your staff with the right systems
3. Celebrate and take responsibility for staff

This essay explores these three elements, arguing that ethos, teaching, achievement and behaviour will be most successful when both teachers and support staff are cherished. I hope other schools may find some of these ideas useful. Many of our ideas come from other schools, and it is only thanks to them that we are succeeding so far.

## 1. Trust your staff to do a good job

Not all schools can do this, of course. In fact, a school in difficulty really shouldn't do this at all. Senior teams in those schools first need to figure out who can be trusted to perform well, and who cannot. However, a luxury of starting off from scratch is that one can hire who one wants, and I have put real effort into picking the right people. So far, so good. That's an understatement. My staff are extraordinary and I thank my lucky stars every day that I've managed to find them.

### Recruitment

I've always thought recruitment is the most difficult part of leadership in schools. Recruitment is hard because judging someone on an interview isn't easy. One has to have the nerve to hold out for what one wants. We've just been hiring for next September. We'll see how things work out, but the new appointees look pretty damn good and I am optimistic. We haven't had a Music teacher this year at all. We advertised four times. We have only just appointed our Head of Music who will begin in September. Our excellent Head of Art didn't start until January this year.

Some parents were concerned. We had promised a curriculum including Art and Music and we began in September without either. But I pointed out to them that we could have hired Art and Music teachers, and parents would have been satisfied seeing someone in the role, however good they may have been. But we don't appoint to just fill holes. Sometimes people say when interviewing that they appoint the person who performs best on the day. We don't. We try to appoint the right person for the job and the school. Sometimes that means waiting.

My teachers are all here because they have very high standards. They weren't just appointed because they happened to apply at the right time, or performed best on the day. They got the job because they fit with the school, and have what it takes to be part of the Michaela family.

### Watch the bureaucracy

When you get it right on hiring restless, talented teachers who are interested in changing the world of education, you can then trust them to do just that. As a Head, you only need to jump in when there are problems. When staff are given autonomy and responsibility, they'll fly with it. They'll also enjoy it.

Our 'knowledge' teaching makes us different. We are very proud of lessons that some people might find old-fashioned. We teach facts unapologetically. We teach children to learn things by heart. When people who don't understand your school's ethos are critical of staff (including Ofsted inspectors), don't allow them to weaken your belief in what is right. If you think your staff are fantastic, then guard that opinion in the face of all opposition, until you can prove how right you are with national results.

Of course, this does take a certain amount of confidence in one's ability to appoint. But what is the alternative? Watching staff like hawks? Does that really ever work? Anything that looks like bureaucracy is bureaucracy. When in doubt, run a mile. That is why, at Michaela, we follow some simple rules:

- No grading or high-pressured observations
- No individual lesson plans
- No expectations of all-singing-and-dancing lessons
- No starters/plenaries/group work/attention grabbers/whizzy nonsense/ mystery/lesson objectives
- No expectation to demonstrate progress within a single lesson
- No unnecessary manual data input or unnecessary paperwork
- No IT expectations
- No expectation of setting and marking homework – it is centralised
- No time-wasting, temporary display
- No performance-related pay or divisive bonuses

We don't do these things because they aren't good for staff well-being, and because they aren't good for the pupils. Do these things really raise achievement? Do they make staff into better teachers? Those are the questions one needs to ask every time a decision is made.

If you ever catch yourself with a tick list, you need to ask yourself if it is necessary. I have wasted countless hours over my lifetime doing brainless school bureaucratic tasks that made little difference to anyone, except to tick a box to make some senior manager happy. So we listen to our teachers. We think about every admin task we ask them for and consider whether it is really necessary. And we ask ourselves whether the impact justifies the energy expended.

## No graded observations

I have never known a member of an ST who enjoys doing graded observations. This is because they are relatively unsure about grading, feel uncomfortable giving out grades for lessons where the subject isn't their expertise, and deep down they know setting targets twice a year from observing one lesson is absurd.

Graded observations provide little insight as to how a teacher teaches day in, day out. The observation means that the teacher performs to the observer, showing the observer things that he or she would never normally do. It is simply impossible to both judge a lesson with a grade and to see something normal. And 'normal', after all, is what Heads should want to see. Grading lessons in preparation for an Ofsted visit is different and perhaps worthwhile if, as a school, one values the Ofsted stamp.

Because then one really is teaching staff to simply perform for the inspectors. One isn't judging their quality as teachers.

## No lesson plans

Writing individual plans for single lessons is a waste of teachers' time. Plan for the week, for the month, for the year, but planning for a lesson should always be done lightly. Mastery and memory over time should be one's objective as a teacher and as a school.

At Michaela, we have an open door policy where anyone can wander in and out of lessons. I don't really notice if the teacher is standing or sitting, whether they are using a PowerPoint or not, or whether the teacher has his lesson plan written down in front of him. I would be quite worried if I saw group work, or lots of movement of children around the room. Anything whizzy would make me raise an eyebrow, and the constant explanation of where children are and where they are going would tell me that we, the ST, had failed in establishing our ethos around the school. But I never see any of this nonsense from my staff. They get what our school is about, they embrace the autonomy they are given, and they run with it.

## Minimal marking

As for marking, I tell staff to stop marking so much. Yes, that's right. We feed back to pupils from the front of the class to all of the pupils. Do we believe in 'personalising learning'? No. Do we believe in staff spending countless hours writing three personalised targets in books where they are essentially writing the same thing over and over (because so often children make the same mistakes) but then trying to phrase it differently each time so that at the next 'book look' one's targets will look as personal as possible? Erm, no.

I have better things to do. So do my staff. And our pupils have better things to do than to pretend to read targets which they can then pretend to act on. Far better to have a teacher clearly instruct a whole class on how to improve, then insist that they do it.

Much of our continuous assessment is carried out by weekly quizzes that get marked automatically by the bespoke IT system we had built for us. This is proving to be a simple way for teachers to keep an eye on progress and learning, without lots of marking.

## Minimal display

I admit I took some convincing on this one. Should staff spend days and days doing colourful displays of pupils' work? The week before the Year 6 parents' open evening, children in lessons are colouring away. Then hours and hours are whiled away pinning them up on pin boards, after having spent further time cutting out backing paper and that funny shiny corrugated border stuff that makes a pin board look rather lovely.

But why are we doing this? Because it looks nice. Never mind that it wastes learning time and undermines any school's ethos of high expectations of the children. The fact there is something lovely about having the children's work up on the walls means that no-one ever questions whether display is a useful thing to do.

It isn't. We've saved our teachers so much time by not requiring it. Instead, we have framed pictures of beautiful pieces of art, from actual artists with a small write-up next to them to explain something about the artist. All decisions at Michaela are made with this key thought in mind: Does the effort put in by staff justify the end result? The end result may be 'nice', but 'nice' simply isn't good enough to warrant spending lots of teacher time on it.

## 2. Support your staff with the right systems

### Centralised homework

Homework is a constant stress for teachers. First of all it is hard to think of what to set and be consistent. Finish off class work one day and the next it is a pre-prepared worksheet. Then how do you get it all in? Was little Johnny absent when you set the homework? Can you remember? Even the best teachers who chase homework relentlessly (and that is exhausting and time consuming) never get it all in. And that means within-school-variation, a curse of many schools, so we try to reduce it at all costs in every domain. It means pupils generally complete homework for Mr X because he chases them, but often don't for Miss Y because she's new and is too busy chasing behaviour to chase homework.

So we took the idea of centralised reading logs, used by a number of schools now, starting I believe at King Solomon Academy, and expanded it. Homework at Michaela is centralised and consists of reading logs which require pupils to read every night; completing set tasks on the IXL Maths website; and self-quizzing in preparation for knowledge tests back at school: always the same three things every evening. Parents find it easy to support because it is always the same and there is no within-school-variation both at school and at home. Both staff and parents are supported.

Of course, the reason we can have self-quizzing as the main body of homework for all subjects at Michaela is because we believe in memory and mastery. As I have said, we teach a knowledge curriculum. We firmly believe that if it hasn't been committed to memory, then it hasn't been learned. When homework is about learning things by heart, it can be centralised and marking is greatly reduced. With all homework centralised, it generally gets done. And if it doesn't, the pupil receives a centralised detention.

### Centralised detentions

Detentions and the different ways teachers handle them are another major source of within-school-variation and therefore division in schools. Some teachers chase the pupils who don't show, others go and get them and escort them to the detention room, while others have enough respect to just wait until they arrive and tick them off as they do. The more this takes place, the more the teachers are set against each other.

When detentions are centralised, pupils tend to go. We have two detentions per day, at lunch and after school to ensure there is an immediate sanction felt by the pupil. The whole school is set up in such a way as to ensure the detention system works. No child ever escapes detention or a consequence for missing one.

## Within-school-variation

Whose fault is it if the pupils have more respect for Miss X than they do for Mr Y? It is a complex question. Often, the teachers feel that it is the ST's fault: they aren't in the corridors supporting enough, they aren't strict enough, they don't back staff enough. And equally, STs feel that Mr Y would be just fine if only he turned up at his classroom door early, taught more engaging lessons, and built relationships with the pupils.

There is normally truth on both sides. But ultimately, if you're a leader and things are going wrong, the fault is yours by definition. It is for you to fix it. If support and help make little difference, then it is your duty to move that member of staff on. Leaders need to take responsibility. They also need to ensure systems are in place that are supportive of staff and reduce within-school-variation.

## Consistency

Children like routine. The more routinised basic classroom practices become, the more time children have to spend learning. So how does one reduce within-school-variation as much as possible? By ensuring staff teach in a consistent way. Our staff all make pupils use rulers to read anything, all number lines on a page, all use 'go' as the key word to set the pupils off on task, all use 'slant'[i] as the call to attention, all use 'track' to get pupils to look at them, all count down from five when pupils are handing out the books. Staff pop in and out of each other's lessons to increase that consistency.

When timetabling, we try to reduce movement around the school as much as possible. No split timetabling and no two-week timetables. We also make sure that no subject ever has less than 2 lessons per week. So we have cut subjects, in the way that Ark Schools do. We do not offer lessons in Information Technology or Design Technology. We believe in depth before breadth.

Because staff well-being is so important, we aim to give teachers their own classroom wherever possible. Like some other schools, we man the toilets, watch the corridors constantly and hope to develop our Future Leaders (prefects) to help us manage corridors next year. With such a strong emphasis on consistency, the biggest challenge that lies ahead for Michaela is how we remain consistent as we grow.

---

i   SLANT is an acronym developed in American Charter Schools to teach pupils positive classroom behaviour. It stands for S– Sit up; L– Listen; A-Ask and answer questions; N– Nod your head (or Never Interrupt at Michaela); T– Track the speaker.

## Culture

I believe King Solomon Academy started the idea of family lunch. Pupils always sit in the same place, serving each other food, handing each other plates and cutlery, clearing up after themselves, as if they were at home around the dinner table. What a great idea it is! Our pupils love it. From Dixons Trinity, we took the idea of appreciations, which are a wonderful tool to teach children how to be grateful and how to understand kindness. Children stand at the end of lunch and clap twice to show they appreciate a piece of kindness someone (a teacher or pupil) has shown them. We promote this family atmosphere across the school.

Staff look after each other and the pupils. Pupils do the same in return. Amazingly, with an intake that is half on pupil premium, and includes some very challenging families, staff are able to leave classroom doors unlocked, leave their iPads and phones out, and we don't have to worry about anyone taking them. This won't last forever, but how wonderful to work in an inner-city school where this is possible!

I believe staff feel looked after at Michaela. We have an extended day, starting at 7:55am and ending at 4pm. It takes its toll. So we asked governors for a two-week half term (an idea also taken from Dixons Trinity) which was approved. In addition, we don't believe in performance-related pay. By definition, if you're looking to hire professional, questioning people, then you aren't looking for those who want to be set a target and rewarded financially for achieving it. PRP undermines everything we believe in, not only from the perspective of encouraging the wrong motivation in teachers, but also in terms of the workload created in having to justify achieved targets.[1]

## 3. Celebrate and take responsibility for staff

It is easy to forget how lucky we are in a free school started from scratch. So we need to keep reminding staff just how fortunate we are to work in a school like ours where pupils open doors for us, ask us how we are, where no-one ever swears or is even rude. We also need to remind pupils and parents how lucky they are, and defend staff when people on the outside don't understand what we're about.

## Teaching pupils

Pupils need to be taught to behave and to be grateful. They need to be taught to concentrate and to have high standards for their learning. Staff need to be taught to never do all-singing and all-dancing lessons where children are entertained rather than taught. Those kinds of lessons really let our children down.

From King Solomon Academy we took the idea of a transition week, which we call Behaviour Bootcamp and we spend the first week in September with Year 7s, teaching them how to behave. It has worked wonders. We remind them constantly of what is possible, guiding their conversations at lunch and pushing them to limits they never knew they could reach. Pupils often thank teachers for their lessons, regularly offer their help and make teachers feel valued. Appreciations at lunch and good postcards from pupils to staff are a couple of the mechanisms that support this ethos.

## Teaching staff

Staff at Michaela can develop into the best teachers they can possibly be. I often look at staff teaching and feel slightly envious. I was never as good a teacher as they are, and I never will be because I don't teach at Michaela now. At Michaela, because of the environment and the supportive systems, teachers can do things they would never imagine doing in some other schools.

We have staff who write educational blogs and are on Twitter, and if you use social media to follow education debates I strongly encourage you to follow them! At first we shied away from such visibility, worried of the consequences. But now we embrace it. Teacher blogs are on the home page of our website inviting everyone to read about what we do at Michaela.

Staff also speak at events like ResearchED, Teach First conferences and the Wellington Festival of Education to tell others about what we do. We say to families that they can visit us any time they want: not just at pre-organised open mornings, but any time they want, to see any part of the school. Guests regularly visit us for lunch with the pupils, from Labour MP and London Mayoral candidate David Lammy, to the philosopher Roger Scruton, to the Conservative Minister for Schools Nick Gibb. We love to celebrate who we are. We want to shout it from the rooftops.

## Ofsted

Ofsted is an unfortunate and difficult hurdle to surmount when trying to keep a handle on work-life balance for staff. It requires a huge amount of work for an 'outstanding', especially if you are a new school and don't have national data to prove outstanding results.

Enormous pressure is felt by STs around the country thanks to Ofsted. Teachers are scared of letting the school down. Tension builds. So much time is spent trying to second guess what sort of performance Ofsted inspectors would like to see when they visit. Because that's all it is: a performance.

The way we've dealt with this is to take 'outstanding' off the table. We don't want it. We want a 'good'. I'm not just saying this. We know what sorts of things might get us an 'outstanding'. Other schools have been very clever in the past at figuring out what is needed to get that grade and getting it. We could copy them. But we won't. We'll do a few things though, to make sure we get a 'Good'. We are aiming at a 'Good'. Why? Because to us, staff well-being matters more than the Ofsted 'outstanding' stamp. Does being told one is 'outstanding' justify the extra work from staff that won't make the school better and in some ways will make it worse? We don't think so.

So we aim for 'Good' and look forward to the day when we have national data that is so beyond good that Ofsted will have no choice but to award us an 'outstanding'. And if any Ofsted inspector says any of our staff is anything less than good because they expect to see all-singing and dancing lessons with no regard to memory, I will hit the roof.

## Conclusion

At Michaela we want what is best for our pupils. We believe that a knowledge rather than a skills based curriculum is best. We also want what is best for our staff and we make this our priority so that, in the end, pupils find continuity and happiness at school.

We think that it is only by teaching a knowledge curriculum that it is possible for a school to move away from the usual frenetic model of 'whatever it takes'. Only when teaching is more efficient, and classrooms are filled with real learning, is it really possible for good teachers to have work-life balance.

We wish the system were more supportive of schools doing what is right by children. We wish we could have avoided the fight for three years to get our school off the ground. We wish the unions could see that all we want is the opportunity to establish a good school where we have the choice to do some things differently.

In October 2010, I gave a speech at the Conservative Party Conference about what I saw as the failures of the education system. I spoke just before Geoffrey Canada, who had flown over from New York for the event. He is now retired, a man for whom I have huge admiration, a man who transformed the streets of Harlem with his Harlem Children's Zone and his charter school Promise Academy. The world of education lost a great leader the day Canada retired. Much of what we do at Michaela is inspired by various charter schools in the US. Our motto, Knowledge is Power, is the same as KIPP's: Knowledge is Power Programme.

Thanks to people like Geoffrey Canada, Michael Gove, Nick Gibb, Sally Coates, Michael Wilshaw, the contributors to this book, schools like King Solomon Academy, Dixons Trinity, Reach Academy, Mossbourne and the big academy chains like Ark, Harris, Oasis and others, things are changing. Due to the freedom both in thought and regulation that comes with academy and free school reforms, there are many remarkable schools around the country challenging all of us to up our game. We are living in exciting times, and at Michaela we hope to be part of these changes.

I can't wait to see what happens next.

### Endnotes

1    Birbalsingh, K., 'Performance-Related Pay Will Be A Débacle', *Standpoint Magazine*, January/ February 2014.

# Qualifications: What constitutes real qualifications reform?

## Dr. Tina Isaacs[i]

When the coalition government took power in 2010 it promised to reform fundamentally post-14 curriculum and qualifications. Looking at the changes it has put into effect five years later it certainly has made deep alterations, although as I argue later in this essay, they are evolutionary – which probably suits most people – rather than revolutionary, which I will suggest at this essay's end. From a secondary teacher or lecturer's point of view, no qualification remains untouched: GCSEs and A-levels have new structure, content and assessment rules; the Diploma has been abandoned; the place of vocational qualifications in performance tables, and therefore in schools at least, has shrunk; EBacc and Progress Eight accountability measures have been established. The following looks at the new qualifications landscape before arguing that if we want true qualifications reform that could suit all 14-19-year-olds we should abandon GCSEs, replacing them, for national standards and school accountability purposes, with what I am calling key stage 4 tests.

## Qualifications reform 2010–2015

In order to understand what has happened in the last five years it is necessary to return briefly to the changes that qualifications underwent as part of Curriculum 2000 and other Labour government qualifications changes. All A-levels became modularised for first teaching in 2000 in order to bring them into line with already modularised vocational qualifications, such as GNVQs, that the government of the day was promoting heavily. New Advanced Subsidiary (AS) qualifications were introduced that were half the size of the full A-level and at the standard of end of first year achievement. There was little in the way of content change, however. GCSEs underwent little significant change at that time; instead their full modularisation took place for qualifications first taught in 2009 and 2010. At the time, most A-levels and GCSEs included coursework or controlled assessment, sometimes as high as 60% internal assessment. In an effort to promote 'parity of esteem' for vocational qualifications, performance tables were expanded to include thousands of vocational qualifications, some the size of four GCSEs, and the government introduced its new flagship vocationally related qualification, the Diploma, which it hoped eventually would rival GCSEs and A-levels in student take-up.[1] The Diploma, available at three levels, covering the GCSE and A-level spectrum contained 10 essential elements: principal learning; project; additional/specialist learning; functional mathematics; functional ICT; functional English (writing); functional English (reading); functional

i    I am grateful to Dr. Paul Newton who worked with me in generating some of the ideas found in this chapter.

English (listening and speaking); personal learning and thinking skills (PLTS); and work experience. Complex grading and awarding arrangements and the inability of many candidates to pass all three functional skills elements were the main sources of the qualification's small take-up and eventual downfall.

Over the ten years from 2000 to 2010, much public dissatisfaction was expressed about the rigour and worthiness of qualifications, with modularisation taking much of the blame because students were taking qualifications in smaller chunks and were able to re-sit modules at least once (GCSE) or an unlimited number of times (A-levels and vocational qualifications). As England's standing in international league tables such as PISA stagnated, concern was also expressed about the level of challenge of the qualifications – were they as complex and demanding as our international competitors' offerings?

The coalition government in 2010 signalled the changes it was going to make to qualifications and why it was going to make them in the Schools White Paper, *The Importance of Teaching*.[2] In terms of post-14 education it set out to:

· Review and reform the National Curriculum
· Encourage schools to offer a broad set of academic subjects to age 16, through a new accountability measure called the English Baccalaureate (EBacc)
· Reform vocational qualifications so that they better supported progression to further and higher education and employment
· Support more young people to continue in education or training to age 18
· Work with Ofqual to ensure that students would be able to choose from a range of high-quality and demanding qualifications that universities and employers valued.[3]

In its own terms, the government has been largely successful in putting into place all of these changes, although not to universal acclaim.

### Reforms to key stage 4 qualifications

Just about everything that could be changed in key stage 4 qualifications has been – or is going to be – changed. Fundamentally, structural and assessment adjustments should follow on from, and fully reflect, curriculum changes. I have argued strongly elsewhere that our qualifications-based system shifts the emphasis from what students should know and be able to do to how many examinations they can pass.[4] And because schools and colleges are accountable for students' performance on those qualifications, there has been less of an emphasis on ensuring that many of those students, especially lower achievers, study a broad array of subjects that provide the grounding necessary to thrive in later life. From the outset, the coalition government seemed to recognise this as a fundamental problem and introduced the EBacc accountability measure, consisting of successful performance (GCSE grade C and above) in English, mathematics, science (later including computer science), history or geography and a language other than English. To my mind the measure did not go far enough, because schools might still hesitate to enter their lowest achievers to these grounding subjects since the students' performance would not add much to the grades A*–C accountability measure. If the system were curriculum driven, then all students would need to take certain subjects up to the age of 16 or 18, although not necessarily in the rigid structures that we have on offer today.

It may be that the introduction of different performance measures for schools, announced in the autumn of 2013, will do more to encourage schools to enter all, or most of their students for subjects that matter most.[5] Alongside severely restricting re-sits and early entry of GCSEs, a new 'Progress Eight' accountability measure has been put forward to help achieve this.

The GCSE re-sit problem was caused by schools encouraging students to take GCSE modules at the earliest possible opportunity in hopes of banking a grade C or above; if the student got below that s/he could re-sit the module. With this practice it was possible that students who might otherwise have achieved grade B, A or A* did not do so because once they had achieved the hallowed grade C they stopped studying the content that module assessed. Early entry for entire qualifications was equally pernicious – where once most students who were entered early for a GCSE were high achievers who might continue studying the subject at a higher level, early entry patterns shifted once GCSEs were essentially modularised, especially in the gateway subjects of mathematics and English for mid-level and lower achievers, once again in hopes of racking up C grades. An Ofsted study found that early entry for English GCSEs started rapidly increasing in 2008 and for mathematics in 2009. By 2011 over 200,000 students took their GCSEs early in each subject, in contrast to 9000 (English) and 24,000 (mathematics) in 2005. Some schools were entering all of their students early.[6] Echoing the Ofsted report, the then Secretary of State, Michael Gove, described early entry as harmful to the interests of students.[7] Concerned that in the summer of 2013 23% of mathematics entries and 10% of English entries had been early (an increase of 39% from 2012 to 2013), he stated that early entrants performed worse overall than those who took their exams later, even taking re-sits into account. He pointed out that for some of those candidates key stage 2 performance would suggest that had they carried on until the end of Year 11 they might have achieved a B or better on these essential subjects.

In order to inhibit early entry for qualifications, since the autumn of 2013 (for 2015 performance tables) results from a student's first entry in English, mathematics, science, history, geography and MFL count toward their school's performance tables (other subjects follow in 2016). This is certainly a good thing, although I worry that individual students who might benefit from re-taking a GCSE because of unanticipated poor results may find their schools unwilling to engage in this risky – for the school, not for the student – strategy.

The Progress Eight measure, to be put in place for performance tables in the summer of 2016, consists of students' outcomes measured across eight subjects: English (double weighted); mathematics (double weighted); three other EBacc subjects; and three additional subjects that can include EBacc subjects or other approved qualifications, including vocational qualifications. Regarding the last, the number of vocational qualifications that can be included has shrunk to just over 100 rather than numbering in the thousands thanks to the recommendations found in Professor Alison Wolf's review of 14-19 vocational qualifications.[8] Since schools will be judged by students' achievements in these same subjects, without grade C cut-off weighing as heavily as in the past, I am hopeful that more will be encouraged to offer a broadly based curriculum for all (or almost all) students.

Accountability measures are only part of the 14-16 qualifications reform panoply; alongside are changes to content, linear rather than modular assessment, a policy decision to downgrade/abolish coursework and a new grading system. With the avowed aim to make GCSEs more rigorous and levelled against our international competitors, subject content was reviewed and revised beginning in 2013. New English and mathematics GCSEs will have first teaching in 2015; the rest of the EBacc subjects follow in 2016. The mathematics qualification is about one third larger than its predecessor and ostensibly more demanding; the government has suggested that schools dedicate more time to mathematics teaching. English language GCSE will award 20% of its marks for accurate spelling, punctuation and grammar; English literature GCSE will demand students read Shakespeare, 19th century novels, Romantic poetry and other 'high quality' fiction and drama. Mathematical content has been increased in the sciences.

Revised qualifications will be linear rather than modular, with end of course assessment only. Students dissatisfied with their grades will need to re-take the entire qualification. This ends a very short-lived experiment with fully modular GCSEs that began only in 2009-2010. It is unlikely that this reversion will be lamented by many, and certainly not by me, since it increased the assessment burden and skewed entry patterns. A more controversial decision was to scrap coursework wherever possible, 100% externally assessing most subjects. Fieldwork in geography, while required to happen, will be assessed solely through exams, science practicals will no longer count toward students' grades. While science organisations such as the Wellcome Trust, Nuffield and the Gatsby Charitable Foundation have criticised the move, stating that what is not assessed is not taught, Ofqual and the examinations boards argue that the new science subject criteria require far more practical experimentation than in the past and that practical skills can successfully be measured in an examination. Certainly, science coursework recently has become stale, predictable and boring; if schools buy into the spirit of the new science GCSEs students will reap the benefits. It's only where schools cut corners that students will suffer.

Lastly a new grading system will be put in place, replacing the A* to G grades with grades 9 (highest) to 1 (lowest). Despite potential problems over introducing a completely new reference point for GCSE achievement, for example, getting employers used to the system, Ofqual believes that the best way to signal higher expectations and increased challenge within the qualifications is to break grading links with past qualifications.[9] In the new system, it is thought that approximately the same numbers of students will get a grade 7 and above as got grades A and A* –

thus leading to an additional grade (9) that 20% of grade 7 and above students will get, which in most cases will be a far smaller number than got A* – and while the old C grade would be the equivalent to grade 4, the policy push is for a grade 5 (upper reaches of old grade C/lower reaches of old grade B) to be recognised as 'passing' performance, signalling increased demand and standards. The implications for this change will be a, possibly temporary, lowering of the 'good pass' rates in 2017 and 2018.

With all of this noise on the wire, it is impossible to tell how the new system will play out. With luck, students will take fewer GCSEs (if only the best eight matter) in more established subjects (the Performance Eight effect) that allow for more teaching and learning time (linear assessment only) and reflect more challenging curriculum (content and grading changes). But as long as accountability measures are the system's main drivers, schools will do what they can to maximise their performance table points, and who can blame them?

### *Reforms to post-16 qualifications*

Mercifully, there have been fewer changes to A-levels, but they are still fundamental ones. In a stark reversal of Curriculum 2000, all A-levels will be assessed in a linear fashion. January assessments were abolished in 2012 as a step in this direction. Linear assessment is meant to encourage deep learning over time, rather than 'learn to forget', and to do away with endless examination preparation and resitting (for example, in 2010, 74% of A-level mathematics students re-sat at least one paper).[10]

While the AS qualification will continue to exist, it will only exist as a qualification in its own right, rather than as the first half of an A-level. While the AS qualifications are designed to be taught alongside A-levels, students who take AS qualifications who want to obtain a full A-level in that subject will be assessed at the end of two years on content including that of the AS-level, essentially examining the same content twice. And because the AS level is assessed at the level of first year performance, the full A-level assessment of that same content will be assessed at second year level through more demanding questions. It is entirely possible that the AS will wither on the vine because of potential teaching time lost to examination preparation (although schools and colleges will doubtless continue to offer some sort of end of first year examinations). However, some universities, such as Cambridge, rely on AS results in making their offers and are unhappy to see the demise of such a useful tool. While I understand the concern about loss of teaching time, I too am concerned about the demise of the AS. It is a useful marker of end of first year performance and students have used their AS results to help them make decisions about what to continue studying through to full A-levels. AS results can also help guide students to which universities to which to apply. But of most concern to me is the potential loss of broader learning – if students are judged on the outcomes of three A-levels for university entrance, will they bother to start out on four subjects, as is the case now?

Once again, the assumption is that coursework is only appropriate if absolutely necessary, for example in art and design qualifications. For subjects that retain coursework, it will be reduced, for example the coursework weighting in English will decrease from 40% to 20%. Science A-levels will be 100% externally assessed, although, as with GCSE, there is a requirement for students to carry out a number of practical experiments.

For more practically oriented students, a level 3 TechBacc is being introduced. This includes a 'Tech Level' (230 of which have already been approved for performance table purposes in areas such as agriculture and horticulture; arts; business; child care; construction; engineering; health; ICT; leisure and tourism; and retail – from well-known awarding bodies such as City & Guilds, Pearson BTEC and OCR Cambridge Diplomas), a level 3 mathematics qualification, and an extended project.[11] Those who remain in full-time education but are not interested in pursuing a TechBacc will need to be involved in coherent programmes of study as defined by the Wolf Review. The raising of participation age to 18, which requires young people participate in education or training, could mean that more young people remain in full time education for longer, but the jury is still out on this and the new rules only require the equivalent of one or two days' study per week.

## Do we need more radical reforms?

To my mind, many of the reforms are heading in the right direction, but they are not going far enough. Professor Michael Young argues persuasively about the concept of 'powerful knowledge' to which all students are entitled, regardless of whether or not they find such knowledge difficult to acquire. It is discipline-based, specialised (as opposed to general) and different from the everyday knowledge that students bring to school with them. The National Curriculum, he contends, should be limited to the key concepts in core subjects, thus allowing for greater autonomy in schools, and crucially, assessment should concentrate on feedback about students' performance rather than as an accountability driver.[12] The current reforms lean too heavily on accountability at the expense of feedback on progress, which is the main vehicle for understanding deeply what students have mastered, what they need to continue to work on further and how to go about filling the gaps. Since students' future progression depends almost entirely on the outcomes of their performance on assessments during their upper secondary school and college experiences, I would like to put forward an alternative, concentrating on key stage 4 but with implications for the 14-19 spectrum that, while giving accountability its due, does not make it the be-all and end-all of secondary education.

First, a few premises. National testing, done judiciously and well, can make an important contribution to education and society – it can inform us in a broad manner about students' progress (although continuous assessment by education professionals can be more informative) and ensure that fundamental concepts get taught. However, we have developed highly complex examining structures that are expected to fulfil an extremely large number of educational and social functions.[13] Accountability functions that are based on examination outcomes encourage perverse incentives for participants to undermine the integrity of educational systems by exploiting their weakest links in an attempt to maximise outcomes.[14] This can lead to system failures such as the Curriculum 2000 and GCSE English 2012 'crises'.[15] How can we minimise further system failure and the loss of public confidence that ensues while at the same time ensuring that students have access to powerful knowledge?

I think that part of the answer is reducing the pressure on the examination system by reducing its complexity, reducing the expectations we put on examinations and minimising perverse incentives that can undermine their integrity. This is especially a problem for GCSEs.

There are GCSE examinations in over 70 subjects, offered by five different examination boards. Although current reforms will reinstate the linear, end-of-course examination structure, certain subjects will still be examined more than once a year (mathematics and English). GCSE results are used for so many purposes that their principal purpose seems to have been lost in the mist. Are they primarily for:

- predicting which students will be most successful in a further course of study and selecting between them?
- deciding whether students are sufficiently qualified in a subject?
- deciding which school to send a child to, based on overall GCSE results?
- ascertaining, for accountability purposes, whether the performance of individual teachers, classes or schools is rising or falling relative to targets?
- deciding where to allocate limited resources?
- deciding whether to intervene in a school's running, potentially to the point of shutting it down?
- judging the success of national policy initiatives, in terms of the national results profile?
- enabling examination boards to establish comparable standards in A-level examinations?
- or any of a range of additional purposes?

There is a strong value-for-money argument for using a single set of examination results for multiple purposes. Yet, it is also the case that results that are fit for one purpose may be less fit for another and might be entirely unfit for yet another. In fact, there is very limited evidence of fitness-for-purpose in relation to any of these uses. However, it is widely accepted that: 'the more purposes a single assessment aims to serve, the more each purpose will be compromised'.[16]

The most contentious uses are for accountability. Because GCSE results are used to judge both individual teachers and the schools in which they teach, there is every incentive (and very few disincentives) for teachers to 'cheat' by:

- narrowing down the curriculum to only that which is tested.
- concentrating on certain students to get them above accountability thresholds.

- relaxing official 'controls' over the production of internally assessed work, for example, failing to supervise, or providing too much guidance and feedback.
- drilling students in 'shallow' tactics for answering questions from past papers, rather than teaching for 'deeper' and more robust understanding.
- inflating marks for internally assessed elements in such a way as to ensure that students achieve a particular overall grade.

There are various ways in which progress could be made toward reducing complexity, making expectations more realistic and minimising perverse incentives. We could target some of the more controversial aspects of present arrangements, for example only assessing externally when there is a very strong justification for doing so. Some formal external assessments, at important transition points are necessary, mainly to support accountability purposes (for example key stage 2 tests at the end of primary school). However, where external assessment adds little to internal assessment, or when wholly external assessment is simply not feasible, perhaps we should not attempt to do so.

In addition, we could abandon the presumption that Year 11 students should be examined across a large suite of general qualifications. Now that the age of participation in education or training has been raised to 18, there is little to justify 16-year-olds taking a plethora of general qualifications – sometimes as many as 13, but usually around eight or nine. In line with the notion of only assessing externally when there is a very strong justification, I recognise the widespread desire for some formal external assessment at 16, to support secondary school accountability purposes. However, I do not believe that this purpose is best served by current external qualifications. We could abandon the GCSE examination and, for accountability purposes, introduce instead a small set of National Curriculum tests to be sat at the end of key stage 4. This core set would include English and mathematics and perhaps other subjects (for example, some or all of the EBacc subjects). The tests could be developed by an independent agency, similar to the Standards and Testing Agency that operates in England now, but free from government interference.

To ensure all students get the opportunity to study powerful knowledge, it would be compulsory to study the EBacc subjects at least until age 16; other subjects would be optional, and would be assessed internally. For those subjects tested, the external results should be complemented by teacher/lecturer judgement, based on continuous assessment across the entire course, much in the way that New York State has a battery of curriculum-based Regents examinations that count for part of a student's grade point average (GPA), complemented by teacher judgement, which also figures in to the GPA.[17] Fewer tests naturally entail smaller costs, but more importantly return the focus to curriculum rather than qualifications. It is important to note that internal assessment would work only as long as schools and teachers were not held directly accountable in a punitive way for their results from key stage 3 onwards. An even more radical alternative would be only to test English and mathematics *at* age 16, with the remaining tests to be taken *by* age 18, allowing weaker students continued access to core subjects. Another alternative would be the

Scandinavian model, where students must prepare for testing in all of the subjects but only two or three subjects would be tested each year on a rotating (and as random as possible) basis.

These recommendations represent major sacrifices. Yet, to borrow the 'lifeboat' game metaphor: when the lifeboat is sinking, the unacceptable compromise of which family members to save becomes very real indeed. To avoid our test and examination systems sinking, we need to take evasive action. If we are prepared to make sacrifices like these, then we might be able to re-orient the system to promote good teaching and learning.

I am aware that by maintaining even a few tests for accountability purposes could continue the perverse incentives to game the system and that measures would need to be put in place to develop 'tests worth teaching to' (no easy feat) and to de-emphasise as much as possible cut-off points and targets. The resultant systems may give the appearance of being somewhat less useful than at present; in the sense, for instance, of serving fewer societal functions. However, many of the societal functions that would *appear* to be served less well, or not at all, are actually not served well by our current systems. Moreover, in relation to the functions that would explicitly be preserved, they could be more transparent, more robust, less expensive, and more likely to inspire public confidence.

## Endnotes

1   Isaacs, T. (2013) 'The Diploma qualification in England: an avoidable failure?', *Journal of Vocational Education and Training*, 65, 2, pp 277–290.

2   Department for Education (2010) *The importance of teaching: the schools white paper 2010* www. gov.uk/government/publications/the-importance-of-teaching-the-schools-white-paper- 2010 [accessed March, 2015].

3   Department for Education (2014), *The Technical Baccalaureate Performance Table Measure* www. gov.uk/government/publications/technical-baccalaureate-measure-for-16-to-19-year-olds [accessed March, 2015].

4   Isaacs, T. 'What Does Good Upper Secondary Education for the Tail – and Maybe Everyone – Look Like?' in Marshall, P. (ed.) (2013) *The Tail*, London, Profile Books.

5   Department for Education (2013) *Changes to early entry at* GCSE www.gov.uk/government/news/ changes-to-early-entry-at-gcse [accessed March, 2015].

6   Ofsted (2013) *Schools' use of early entry to GCSE examinations* www.ofsted.gov.uk/resources/ schools-use-of-early-entry-gcse-examinations [accessed March, 2015].

7   Department for Education (2013) *Changes to early entry at* GCSE.

8   Wolf, A. (2011) *Review of Vocational Education: The Wolf Report*, Department for Education.

9   BMG Research (2013) *New GCSE Grades Research Amongst Employers – Prepared for: Ofqual*, pp 2–3; Long, R. (2014) *GCSE, AS and A Level Reform Standard Note: SN/SP/6962*, London, House of Commons Library.

10  Long, R. (2014).

11  Department for Education (2014).

12  Young, M. (2013) 'Overcoming the crisis in curriculum theory: a knowledge-based approach' *Journal of curriculum studies*, 45(2), pp 101-118.

13  Newton, P. E. (2007) 'Clarifying the purposes of educational assessment', *Assessment in Education: Principles, Policy & Practice*, 14 (2), pp 149–170.

14  House of Commons Children, Schools and Families Committee (2008). Testing and Assessment. Third Report of Session 2007–08. Volume I. Report, together with formal minutes. HC 169-I. London: TSO Limited; Ofqual (2012). GCSE English 2012. Ofqual/12/5225. Coventry: Office of Qualifications and Examinations Regulation.

15  Isaacs, T. (2014) 'Curriculum and assessment reform gone wrong: the perfect storm of GCSE English', *Curriculum Journal*, 25(1), pp 130-147; Tomlinson, M. (2002) *Inquiry into A level standards: Final Report*, Department for Education.

16  Pelligrino, J., Chudowsky, N., and Glaser, R. (2001) *Knowing what students know: The science and design of educational assessment*, Washington, DC, National Academy Press.

17  Isaacs, T. (2014) '150 years of statewide assessment in New York: are the Regents examinations still fit for purpose?', *Assessment in Education: Principles, Policy & Practice*, 21 (3), pp 344-357.

# Assessment:
# High stakes, low improvement

## Daisy Christodoulou

### Assessment: the national context

The last five years have seen significant reforms to educational assessment in England. Many of the reforms have involved changes to the structure and content of national examinations: GCSE and A-level content has been revised, the grading system for GCSEs has changed, school accountability measures have been redesigned, and in many qualifications, coursework and controlled assessment tasks have been reduced or even abolished. As well as this, the revision of the National Curriculum has led to the removal of National Curriculum levels. The National Curriculum levels describe performance at different stages of achievement, and are used in classroom assessment and in national tests. They are not being replaced; instead, the government have left it to schools to design their own internal assessment systems.

These significant changes to assessment place a new responsibility on schools. Unfortunately, there is some evidence that teacher training and development is not giving teachers and schools the help they need in this area. The recent Carter Review of Initial Teacher Training found that training and development in assessment was particularly weak. Similarly, over the last thirty years, assessment has been used as a lever of government policy with little thought given to what exams are and are not capable of measuring. Greater understanding of some of the basic principles of assessment is vital if we are to avoid some of the mistakes of the past few decades. In the following, I will outline some of these basic principles, the problems that occur when they are ignored, and the implications they have for schools and policy-makers.

### How valuable are exams?

How valuable are exams? What can we learn from them, and how should we use them? Often, debates about the value of exams overlap with debates about the value of academic achievement. As a result, many criticisms of examinations are criticisms of academic achievement; that is, the objection is not to exams *per se*, but to the kinds of things they measure. Take, for example, AS Neill, arguing that:

> If we have to have an exam at eleven, let us make it one for humour, sincerity, imagination, character – and where is the examiner who could test such qualities?[1]

By contrast, those of us who think that academic achievement is vitally important often feel that in order to defend academic achievement, we must therefore defend the use of exams. And so, up to a point, we must. Exams are valuable and tell us many useful things. Historically, they have helped to curb nepotism and promote meritocracy. No developed country in the world makes do without exams, and their use extends well beyond the school gates. We all feel happier knowing pilots and surgeons have passed them.

However, it must be remembered that exams are only proxies for academic achievement. This means that methods which increase exam scores may not necessarily increase academic achievement. It also means that in the debate about the value of exams, it is possible to criticise the way exams are used at the moment without criticising the value of academic achievement. Indeed, my argument here is that over the last twenty years, some particularly damaging uses of exams have actually impeded academic achievement.

## Has holding schools accountable for exam results raised standards?

Since the early 1990s, schools have been measured and judged by the results their pupils get in national examinations. Primary schools are ranked by the proportion of their year 6 pupils who achieve level 4, and secondaries by the proportion of year 11s who achieve 5 A*-C GCSE grades, including English and maths. The theory behind the introduction of these league tables was that naming and shaming schools with low performance would result in them raising their game and delivering a better education for their pupils. On the surface, that is exactly what has happened. In 1995, only 44% of pupils got 5 A*-Cs at GCSE. In 2011, 80% did. On this reading, exam-based accountability has been a triumphant success. Set the target, set the incentives and punishments, and you will get the results you want.

Except, of course, it isn't that simple. Whilst grades on national exams have improved, evidence from a wide range of other sources suggests that standards have not improved. International surveys such as PISA and TIMSS suggest that pupil performance over this period has stagnated, or perhaps increased or decreased a little. Other independent studies have more in common with the PISA and TIMSS surveys than the results from national exams.[2] Rob Coe, Professor of Education at Durham University, has compared the results from all these different sources and concluded that 'the extent to which rising GCSE grades can be interpreted as evidence of rising standards seems very problematic.'[3]

What is the solution to this anomaly? How can GCSE grades have improved so dramatically, and performance on other tests improved so little? One plausible interpretation of this anomaly is that we are seeing an example of Goodhart's Law in action. Goodhart's Law, named after a former Bank of England economist, holds that when a measure becomes a target, it loses value as a measure. It is a frequent flaw in high-stakes accountability systems. When you attach particularly high stakes to any measure, the risk is that the measure in question gets distorted. So, for example, the main target secondary schools were held accountable to was the proportion of pupils achieving 5 A*-C grades including English and maths at GCSE. By focussing on pupils very near the C/D grade threshold, schools were able to improve their performance on the target without actually improving education for all of the pupils in the school.[4]

Goodhart's Law was coined in response to the distortion caused by economic targets, and has since been applied to many different sectors. In healthcare, a UK government target for A&E patients to be seen within four hours led to patients being held in ambulances outside hospitals in order to avoid 'starting the clock'.[5] Similarly, a US survey showed that targets based on mortality rates after surgery affect doctors' clinical decisions about whether to perform surgery or not.[6] Target-based accountability in any sector is problematic. However, it is even more problematic in education because of the nature of educational measurement. As already mentioned, exams are not direct measures of academic achievement. If it is possible for targets based on something as precise, definite and easy to measure as mortality to cause distortions, how many more problems will there be with targets based on more indirect and imprecise measures like exam grades?

## What do exams measure?

That exam scores are indirect measures is one of the most fundamental but poorly understood principles of assessment. Put simply, the scores an individual pupil gets on a test do not matter in and of themselves. Dylan Wiliam explains it like this:

> The really important idea here is that we are hardly ever interested in how well a student did on a particular assessment. What we are interested in is what we can say, from that evidence, about what the student can do in other situations, at other times, in other contexts. Some conclusions are warranted on the basis of the results of the assessment, and others are not. The process of establishing which kinds of conclusions are warranted and which are not is called validation and it is, quite simply, the central concept in assessment.[7]

Daniel Koretz, an American professor of assessment, puts it in these terms:

> Test scores reflect a small sample of behaviour and are valuable only insofar as they support conclusions about the larger domains of interest. This is perhaps the most fundamental principle of achievement testing.[8]

What matters is not the test, but the inferences the test allow us to make. It is a simple principle with far-reaching implications.

In explaining how tests work, Koretz uses opinion polls as an analogy. These polls ask a sample of people about their views on an issue and make assumptions about the views of the entire population based on this. Often, the sample is very small in comparison to the wider population; it is not unusual to find opinion polls making accurate inferences about the views of 40 million voters based on a sample of just a thousand voters. In this case, the views of the 1,000 voters are the sample, and the views of the 40 million are the wider domain. In the case of a maths test, for example, the questions on the test itself are the sample, and the pupil's entire mathematical understanding is the domain. In the case of a vocabulary test, the questions on the test itself are the sample, and the pupil's entire vocabulary is the domain. In all these cases, we are not actually interested in the information from the sample in and of itself. The sample only matters if it can tell us something about the domain. When we look at a pupil's results from that maths results, we expect it to tell us more than just how they performed on those particular questions at that particular moment in time. We expect it to tell us something much wider about that pupil's general mathematical understanding.

In short, tests sample a small part of what a pupil knows and can do, and the results are intended to indicate all of what she knows and can do. This means that the test scores are not actually important in and of themselves. They only matter in that they allow you to make a judgment about the entire domain.

This point may seem obvious but too many school improvement strategies do not take it into account. Improvements on the exam sample, however they have been achieved, are automatically seen as improvements in the domain. Koretz gives an example of a US principal who argued that her school's excellent test scores had been achieved by teaching to the test, but that this was fine because the test was measuring valuable skills and knowledge. Koretz goes so far as to call this argument 'nonsense'.[9] Even if the individual questions are testing valuable skills, what actually matters is not those questions but the inference we can make from them. If instruction has been geared towards the types of questions found on the test, that inevitably weakens the inference we can make about performance on the wider domain, which in the end is the only thing about the test score that actually matters.

In the UK, we see a similar misunderstanding of this vital point. One common response to England's improved GCSE scores but stagnant PISA scores is to claim that it is because pupils hadn't been taught to the PISA tests. The head of PiXL, the school improvement organisation, has suggested that the difference between the GCSE and PISA scores can be explained by the fact that pupils are not taught to the PISA tests: if we want to improve on the PISA tests, then we should direct instruction to them.[10] But the PISA tests of mathematics, literacy and science are drawing from the same domains as the GCSEs in those subjects. If pupils are performing a lot better on the latter than the former, it calls into question the validity of those results. As Koretz argues, the 'acid test' which determines if forms of test preparation are legitimate or not is whether the gains from it generalise to other tests or not. 'Gains that are specific to a particular test...are worthless'.[11]

## What is teaching to the test and why is it so damaging?

With this principle in mind, which kinds of test preparation result in false gains? I'd like to consider two: first, excessive focus on the exam sample, and, second, neglect of items in the wider domain.

Excessive focus on technical details of the exam rubric and typical question structures will lead to gains that are specific to that particular test. Of course, a certain amount of familiarity with the rubric is required, which is why one or maybe two mock exams are valuable. Beyond that, however, any gains from this method are very unlikely to generalise to other tests of the same domain. Analysis of popular textbooks can show us how widespread this approach is. Three major exam boards offer a history

GCSE unit on Germany from 1919-1945, but no generic textbook covers this period. Instead, the Schools History Project has produced three different textbooks, one for each exam board.[12] Each textbook includes almost as much information on exam structure as it does on the history of Germany, with 'Meet the Examiner' sections breaking up the text, and large features on 'the 8 mark question 1' and 'answering change questions'. This is not an isolated example: an analysis of textbooks by Tim Oates showed the most popular ones were characterised by 'highly instrumental approaches to learning, oriented towards obtaining specific examination grades'.[13]

As we've seen, performance on the test sample is only valid if it gives you an inference about the domain. If items from the wider domain are not taught, this will obviously weaken the inference. For example, when beginning a history unit on Germany 1919-1945, a teacher may decide that a week or two doing some background study on 19th century Germany would be useful. Although no question on that topic would feature on the exam, it would indirectly help pupils' understanding of the exam topic. However, where the focus is on teaching to the test, this is just the type of activity which gets cut. Again, the popular textbooks bear this out: although they feature many pages of 'Meet the Examiner' style advice, the First World War is barely mentioned. This is perhaps understandable given that it is a topic on the National Curriculum in previous school years. However, 19th century Germany is not mentioned either, and this is not likely to have been studied in previous years. Clearly, to understand Germany from 1919-1945 it's more important to meet the examiner than to meet Bismarck.

## Can coursework solve this problem?

On the surface, coursework seems to solve the sample and domain problem. If the problem with exams is that they cannot measure the whole domain, but can only sample, then coursework appears to offer a solution, as it allows for several samples from the domain. However, actually the reverse is true, because coursework tasks are set in advance and known by the teacher, and sometimes the pupils too, ahead of teaching. This makes it much easier to direct teaching towards the precise task on the coursework paper. In practice, therefore, the two problems outlined above are seen most acutely in coursework tasks. Consider the example of a pupil who reads the first chapter of *Great Expectations* and then writes a coursework essay on the way the author builds suspense in the first chapter. Compare that with a pupil who reads the entire novel and revises for an exam on it. This pupil receives the same question, and writes an essay of similar quality to the coursework pupil. However, the essay the exam pupil writes will clearly be able to support many more meaningful inferences about the pupil's achievement than the essay the coursework pupil has produced.

## The problems with National Curriculum levels

National curriculum levels were another important part of the education reforms of the early 1990s, and they exacerbated many of the problems outlined above. Their use distorted classroom practice, and also misrepresented pupil performance.

Levels were used both for internal classroom-based assessment, and for reporting results on national tests. This in itself was unhelpful, as it meant within-lesson assessment was constantly structured and defined in terms of national assessments. Just as Tim Oates found that GCSE textbooks contained few assessment tasks not found in the final exam, so levels encouraged classroom assessment to take the form of terminal exams.

This may not sound like a particularly significant problem, but it had huge educational consequences. Many types of valuable assessments do not lend themselves well to levels. Spelling tests, times tables grids, and short recap quizzes are all valuable for the classroom teacher, but are not capable of being levelled. Such tasks were replaced by activities that could be levelled: often large, exam-style activities. Thus, the use of National Curriculum levels in day-to-day teaching increased the amount of teaching to the test.

As well as distorting formative assessment, National Curriculum levels provided poor quality summative information, for three reasons. First, they were based on prose descriptors. As many educationalists have shown, attempting to define in prose the standard required to achieve a certain level is fiendishly difficult, and often leads to inaccuracies.[14] For example, level descriptors relied on vague adverbs to define achievement: the difference between a level 6 and 7 on the speaking and listening performance descriptor was the difference between speaking 'fluently' and speaking 'confidently'. In some cases, the descriptors merely begged the question: the descriptor for 'exceptional performance' too often consisted of lists of adjectives and adverbs that were essentially synonyms for exceptional. Second, level descriptors suggested that there were fundamental differences between different levels. In actual fact, level boundaries are arbitrary markers on a normal and continuous distribution. The difference between a pupil at the bottom of level 4 and the top of level 3 is far less than the difference between a pupil at the bottom of level 4 and the top of level 4. Combined with pressure from threshold-based league tables, this misconception encouraged schools to coach pupils just below certain levels in order to push them into the next level. If levels really were discrete categories, then coaching pupils to achieve a level 4 might have had some value. When you know that performance is continuous, not discrete, then it is apparent that it is a much more hollow activity. This is a problem with all grade-based systems, but it was exacerbated by the third flaw, which is that the levels were particularly large and therefore particularly unhelpful. At the end of year 6, most pupils are defined by one of just three levels.

Some simple statistics will demonstrate what this meant in practice: research from 1995 showed that a group of seven-year-olds assessed at level 2 had reading ages which varied from 5.7 to 12.9 years.[15] Similarly, in the 2014 KS2 reading tests, 50% of pupils received a level 5, which at this stage is defined as working above national expectations. But if half of all pupils receive this level, there is clearly a vast difference between a pupil at the bottom of level 5 and a pupil near the top. Assuming a normal distribution, their reading ages on a standardised test would probably vary from about 10 to 17. Taken together, therefore, the above three flaws meant that levels obscured and misrepresented pupil performance.

## Some possible solutions

### Better exam design

So how can some of the above problems be solved? Clearly, better exam design would mitigate some of these problems, and some valuable reforms are about to happen. Coursework is being abolished or reduced in many qualifications, which will make teaching to the sample much harder and will reward good teaching to the domain. More could be done: if exam questions are so tricky and technical that pupils need half a textbook's worth of instruction in them, something has gone wrong. Many teachers feel forced into excessive teaching of exam technique because otherwise, candidates with a good grasp of the domain are penalised for not ticking the precise boxes on the mark scheme. Similarly, exam boards should have to do more to prove what types of inferences are and are not valid to make from their exams, perhaps by doing follow-up tests of a sample of pupils six months or a year after the exam itself. However, whilst these improvements would help, there is still a limit to what better test design can do. Tests can only ever be a sample, and no test in existence could bear the many weights placed on it by the current system. Other reforms are needed too.

### More data, fewer targets

Given the problems with Goodhart's Law, it's tempting to conclude that targets should be abolished completely. At this point, it is important to consider the difference between targets and open data. The problems outlined above have been caused more by the former than the latter. In fact, in many cases, the problems of badly-designed targets have been made worse by the lack of open data. For example, if a parent wanted to find out if a school really was focussing excessively on pupils at the C/D borderline, or if they were attempting to improve all pupils' performance equally, some data that might have helped them is a breakdown of individual grades in each subject in the school. Until very recently, this has not been available.[16] When lots of statistics are available, it makes manipulation of individual targets much harder.[i] In the longer run, it would also be helpful to have more diverse analyses of data. Instead of monolithic government targets and the distortions they create, external organisations could look for hidden patterns and trends. The Open Public Services Network have recently published some interesting work looking at areas of the country where sciences and languages are less likely to be offered for study.[17] One of the chairs of the OPSN, Simon Lebus, has said that 'an intelligent mining of data is probably a much more useful tool in improving educational standards than

---

i   In early 2015, the government published individual breakdowns of this type for the first time. They attracted little attention, despite revealing some startling facts: for example, in some schools, all the pupils in the year 11 cohort had on average retaken their maths GCSE a total of 8 times.

the overly mechanical snapshot represented by traditional league tables and the very instrumental approach to education that they encourage."[18]

In the longer term, this would probably be the best solution. In the short term, if we are to have government targets, then they should be designed in a way that avoids as many of the above distortions as possible. The current way exam performance is reported is distorting in three ways. First, pupil performance is reported as a grade, which gives disproportionate weight to marginal changes at grade boundaries. Reporting performance as a scaled score where 100, for example, represents the average, and performance ranges from 65–135, could solve this. Second, school-level targets are based on threshold measures such as the percentage of pupils achieving 5 A* to C grades, or the percentage achieving level 4. Again, as we've seen, these lead to a disproportionate focus on pupils close to the threshold. Reporting school performance as an average could solve this. Finally, reporting raw attainment scores rewards schools whose pupils are high-attaining to begin with, and penalises those whose pupils are not. Reporting value-added scores reduces this problem, although value-added scores are subject to more measurement error than other measures.

Some of these changes are about to happen: at primary, the government have replaced levels with a scaled score, but retained a threshold measure. At secondary, the reverse is the case: grades have been retained, but the school performance measures changed to an average of all pupils' grades based on their best eight GCSE results. In both phases, there are new value-added progress measures as well. The government are unlikely to move away from reporting grades at GCSE, but one relatively simple and powerful reform would be to change the primary target from the planned threshold measure to one based on an average instead. This would reward the progress made by all pupils, and stop the damaging focus on pupils close to the threshold.

### School-led innovation with support from research organisations

National curriculum levels have been abolished, which, given the flaws outlined above, is the right move. Primary test scores will now be reported as a scaled score. However, National Curriculum levels were also used for internal assessment, and it is up to schools to design their own replacements for this function. This will allow formative classroom assessment to be determined by the needs of the teacher and the class. National curriculum levels showed that trying to impose a national assessment structure on all forms of assessment had many unhelpful consequences.

Whilst the general principle of teacher and school-led improvement is a good one, many schools lack the capacity to make these improvements. As we've seen, the recent Carter Review of Initial Teacher Training found that many important assessment concepts, such as validity and criterion-referencing, were simply not being taught.[19] There is no reason why this has to be the case, however: some of the world's leading educational assessment organisations are based in the UK. The National Foundation for Educational Research, the Centre for Evaluation and Monitoring, Cambridge Assessment and GL Assessments are all home to vast amounts of expertise and information on assessment. More links between their researchers and schools could help to build the capacity schools need to design effective replacements for National Curriculum levels.

## What causes better exam performance?

Perhaps the ultimate cause of these problems is that we lack a clear understanding of what causes learning. Over the same period that schools have come under such pressure to improve exam results, they have also been beset by poor advice about how to do so. A recent Sutton Trust report argued that 'there is some evidence that an understanding of what constitutes effective pedagogy – the method and practice of teaching – may not be so widely shared, and even where it is widely shared it may not actually be right.'[20] Education is unfortunately susceptible to neuromyths such as learning styles, and over the past few years Ofsted, the school inspectorate, have endorsed particular teaching styles which have little backing from evidence.[21]

Measuring exam results, or the 'outputs', of education will only lead to improvements if there is clear understanding of the 'inputs' which will cause improvement. In the case of education, we do not have a clear, system-wide understanding of what causes learning. So, it is no surprise that when pressure on outputs is applied, people focus solely on those outputs. Indeed, so great is the confusion that many of the teach-to-the-test tactics outlined above are actually praised and celebrated as best practice. Whilst this is worrying in some ways, in others it is reassuring. Teachers and schools are not deliberately setting out to try and game the system. They are setting out to do the best by their pupils, within a system where there is a great deal of bad and conflicting advice. The ultimate solution to the problems outlined above is a better institutional understanding of what causes learning. This is not a quick fix, nor is it one that can be implemented by government legislation. But as the past thirty years have shown, Acts of Parliament and quick fixes sometimes create more problems than they solve.

### Endnotes

1   Quoted in Knowles, E. M. (ed.) (1999) *The Oxford dictionary of quotations*, Oxford University Press, p. 540.

2   Coe, R. (2013) *Improving education: a triumph of hope over experience*, Centre for Evaluation and Monitering, p.7.

3   Ibid, p.7.

4   Mansell, W. (2007) *Education by numbers*, London: Politicos Publishing, chapter 8.

5   The King's Fund, 'Have targets improved NHS performance?' (2010). www.kingsfund.org.uk/projects/general-election-2010/key-election-questions/performance-targets [accessed 6 March 2015].

6   Santora, M. 'Cardiologists say rankings sway choices on surgery', *New York Times*, 11 January 2005.

7   Wiliam, D. (2014) *Redesigning schooling: principled assessment design*, Specialist Schools and Academies Trust, p.22.

8 Koretz, D. M. (2008) *Measuring up*, Harvard University Press, pp. 21-22.

9 Ibid, p.254.

10 Stewart, W. 'England must better prepare pupils for Pisa tests to improve its ranking, heads' leader says', *TES*, 2 December 2013.

11 Koretz (2008), p.258.

12 Culpin, C. and Banham, D. (2011) *AQA Germany 1919-1945 for SHP GCSE*, Hodder Education; Culpin, C. and Banham, D. (2011) *Edexcel Germany 1919-1945 for SHP GCSE*, Hodder Education; Culpin, C. and Banham, D. (2011) *OCR Germany 1919-1945 for SHP GCSE*, Hodder Education.

13 Oates, T. (2014) 'Why textbooks count', Cambridge Assessment, p.6.

14 Oates, T. 'How our exam system really functions', *School House Magazine*, 2010 schoolhousemagazine.co.uk/education/examinations/how-our-exam-system-really-functions [accessed 3 March 2015]; Bambrick-Santoyo, P. (2010) *Driven by data: A practical guide to improve instruction*, John Wiley & Sons; Wiliam (2014), p.65.

15 Davies, J., Brember, I. and Pumfrey, P. 'The first and second reading Standard Assessment Tasks at Key Stage 1: a comparison based on a five school study', *Journal of Research in reading* 18.1 (1995), pp. 1-9.

16 Department for Education, '2014 16-18 qualification and subject level results', www.education. gov.uk/schools/performance/download_data.html [accessed 10 April 2015].

17 Open Public Services Network, 'Lack of options: How a pupil's academic choices are affected by where they live', 2015. www.thersa.org/discover/publications-and-articles/reports/lack-of-options-how-a-pupils-academic-choices-are-affected-by-where-they-live/ [accessed 3 March 2015].

18 Lebus, Simon. 'A better path for the future', 2015. www.cambridgeassessment.org.uk/blog/blog-league-tables-better-path/ [accessed 3 March 2015].

19 Carter, A. (2015), 'Carter review of initial teacher training', Department for Education, p.9.

20 Coe, R, *et al* (2014) 'What makes great teaching? Review of the underpinning research', Sutton Trust, p.8.

21 See Waldegrave, H, and Simons, J. (2014) *Watching the watchmen: The future of school inspections in England*, Policy Exchange; Peal, R. (2014) *Playing the Game: The enduring influence of the preferred Ofsted teaching style*, Civitas.

# Social media: Did blogs break the Blob?

## Andrew Old

Michael Gove's tenure as Education Secretary saw dramatic changes in the administration of the education system. From my point of view as a classroom teacher, however, some of the biggest changes were in an opening up of an educational debate. Immediately prior to 2010, there seemed to be a consensus about the aims and methods of education, built around the DCSF, the National Strategies, the GTC(E), the QCDA and Ofsted. The aims were generally broad, going far beyond, and even marginalising the academic. The methods were progressive, emphasising group-work, discussion and ideas generated by students; they were critical of too much teacher direction.

For those of us in the teaching profession who disagreed, particularly because our philosophy and methods were more traditional, dissent was extremely difficult. Organisations who governed us, regulated us, represented us, and claimed to provide expertise about teaching, told us not only that we were wrong, but that if we disagreed we were not doing our jobs correctly. After 2010, all of the above organisations were either reformed or abolished, with only the DCSF (renamed the DfE) and Ofsted (under new leadership) surviving.

As this happened, a variety of ideas, particularly those based around the teaching of knowledge and the greater use of direct instruction, entered (or re-entered) public debate about education. One cause of this change in educational discourse, and possible influence in education policy more generally, was the increasing influence of social media, particularly blogs and Twitter. Social media provided a unique outlet those who had felt that their opinions were being marginalised to speak out, often anonymously, and to share arguments and accounts of what was happening in schools.

I have counted there to be 1273[i] active UK education blogs.[1] While many are obscure and rarely updated, some are widely read and have had a direct influence on education policy. A recent editorial in *The Journal of Philosophy of Education* not only claimed that bloggers were an influence on policy under Michael Gove, it bemoaned their ability to displace established organisations and intellectuals who (in the opinion of the editor) deserved a greater influence on policy.[2]

Having blogged about education since 2006, I have had reason to pay close attention to the potential influence of bloggers over policy throughout that time. Prior to 2010, I can think of no example of an education blogger being credited with influencing policy, or indeed any blogger from the frontline of any public service. The only example I can recall of a minister commenting on a blogger was Home Office

---

i    This includes all blogs that I know to have been written by somebody in or from the UK, and to have been updated in the last six months.

minister Tony McNulty's dismissal of the police blogger, David Copperfield, as "more of a fiction than Dickens" and his later admission that this was said 'inadvertently'.[3]

Michael Gove does not appear to have taken much interest in social media until some time after taking office. One source close to Michael Gove during his time in opposition told me, "blogs (outside of those by journalists) had little impact and twitter none".[4] A blogger, Katharine Birbalsingh, spoke at the Conservative Party conference in October 2010, but her blog became defunct immediately afterwards. Jonathan Simons, who held a number of policy-making roles from May 2010 to late 2011, described the engagement with social media:

> ...the government was still quite dominated by traditional models of engagement in terms of policy-making with engagement via academics, visits to schools, discussions with other civil servants and various great and the good and messages conveyed via the TES. ... I don't recall using social media to test any [initiatives] or even think about ideas or track what was going on, other than really established people like major academics etc.

There was a broad consensus from policy-makers I contacted, including Simons, that there was a subsequent shift and social media came to be seen as an effective way of finding out what was happening in schools. According to Dominic Cummings, who advised Gove in government from 2011 to 2014:

> Blogs had a significant effect on policy and implementation. Two people in particular were influential – Tom Bennett and Andrew Old. A big part of the reason is that because Whitehall is so dysfunctional, it is very hard to know what is really happening on the ground. There are very few reliable information channels to illuminate one's mistakes in a timely way.

Another policy-maker commented that:

> ...new media became very important. Spads [special advisors] and senior policy people read blogs by front line teachers to understand what actually happened in schools. Our press team monitored Twitter not just for opposition or media tweets but for those by teachers. Policy meetings were regularly punctuated by observations gleaned from teachers' blogs.

This is confirmed by former Gove advisor, Sam Freedman (who tweeted prolifically as @Samfr):

> Ministers and advisers read a wide range of blogs when I was in the department and followed debates on Twitter closely ... it's an incredibly useful way of getting information from the ground (though obviously the people on Twitter are not representative of the general teaching profession).

Jonathan Simons, who went on to be head of education at *Policy Exchange*, a think tank with close connections to Michael Gove, contrasted his more recent experiences with his earlier involvement in policy-making:

> From a policy-making perspective now it's basically indispensable. It also helps that

with the advent of smartphones being quite so accessible and also government IT modernising that you can now get twitter on government ICT.

I don't know quite when I'd date the shift from – obviously people including me tweeted a lot in 2010 and 2011, but it didn't really become a continual 24/7 info' and argument flow which it is now... For me it was highly symbolic that Sam [Freedman] tweeted quite so heavily when in government, that marked a big shift, and also interacted with people. But I couldn't place the exact time in which teachers engaged en masse and started having an influence.

That ministers were reading blogs is confirmed by a number of occasions where Michael Gove publicly referenced blogs and bloggers from April 2013, until just before his departure as Education Secretary. In a speech to the NCTL that month, he mentioned a number of bloggers as examples of an increased voice for teachers:

I'm a great fan of Andrew Old, whose brilliant blog *Scenes from the Battleground* provides one of the most insightful commentaries on the current and future curriculum that I've ever read; but I'm also an admirer of John Blake of Labour Teachers, who has transcended party politics to praise all schools which succeed for their pupils, even if they are academies or free schools. I also hugely enjoy the always provocative work of Tom Bennett, the Behaviour Guru, who champions teachers at every turn while challenging them to up their game. And one of the brightest young voices in the education debate is the Birmingham teacher Matthew Hunter,[ii] whose work online and in *Standpoint* magazine reinforces my view that those who are have entered the profession in the last few years – and are entering now – are hugely ambitious for the children in their care.[5]

These bloggers, and others, such as Joe Kirby, were referred to on a number of occasions by Michael Gove as Secretary of State.[6] Usually bloggers were quoted for being teachers who were sympathetic to some of his policies. Sometimes it was mentioned that social media had allowed teachers to enter public debate more easily. In the case of John Blake and I, it was also mentioned that we were Labour Party activists. Of course, this leaves open the question as to whether bloggers were being referenced in order to justify decisions that had already been made, or whether they had actually influenced the decision-making. While bloggers may have influenced the content of Gove's speeches (I was given credit by Gove for providing a memorable example of progressive teaching[7]), this is not the same as influencing a substantial part of policy.

However, the one example where bloggers were most clearly credited with affecting the policy agenda has been over school inspection. Criticism and comment about *Ofsted* in blogs was extensive and suggested that the definite power to make policy within the education system lay more with the inspectorate than with ministers. In a blogpost in August 2014 entitled 'Bloggers lead the campaign to reform Ofsted'[8], Joe Kirby listed 173 blogposts written about Ofsted, including dozens by me. A

---

ii    Pseudonym of Robert Peal

large proportion of these posts centred on how inspectors chose to judge teaching and the evidence that inspectors favoured a more progressive style. However, the pronouncements of the chief inspector Michael Wilshaw, and some of the literature produced after his appointment, repeatedly claimed *Ofsted* recommended no particular style of teaching. Gove publicly declared that such a requirement was in the past:

> ...Ofsted's guidance provided too little clarity about what constituted good teaching; or allowed inspectors' personal prejudices and preferences to be interpreted as 'the Ofsted way'. As a result, and as teacher bloggers like Andrew Old have chronicled, time and again too much emphasis was given to particular practices like group work and discovery learning; while Ofsted inspectors marked teachers down for such heinous crimes as 'talking too much', 'telling pupils things' or 'dominating the discussion'. The good news is that Ofsted – under its inspirational new leadership – is moving to address all these weaknesses and give us a system of inspection of which we can be proud.[9]

A subsequent report in the *Sunday Times* suggested ongoing tensions between ministers and inspectors over criticism of inspectors.[10] Sam Freedman commented that:

> The obvious example [of blogs being a useful source of information] is the stream of blogs on Ofsted looking for particular forms of teaching and the misuse of teacher grading led by [Andrew Old] but contributed to by many others. This led to the department raising the issue with Ofsted [and] to Ofsted prioritising the issue internally.

Similarly, Dominic Cummings elaborated on his claim that blogs had a significant effect on policy and implementation by referring to Ofsted:

> One of the ways in which we could see that what Ofsted said was wrong [was] via blogs like Andrew Old's. To begin with Ofsted tried to ignore them but we would say 'these things are all over the place and they all say the same thing so you can't ignore them'. Gradually, the DfE and even Ofsted had to adapt to the information bubbling up from blogs at the grassroots and the media started paying attention to them too.

Over time Ofsted began engaging with bloggers, while reforming its practices to decrease the emphasis on judging individual lessons. A number of meetings and consultations with bloggers took place. One blogger, David Didau, provided unpaid consultancy when parts of the inspection handbook were rewritten.[11] Additionally, I was given the opportunity to quiz two senior figures in Ofsted live on stage at a ResearchED event in 2014. One of those senior figures, Sean Harford, currently Ofsted's National Director for Schools, acknowledged the effects of social media, while at the same time placing it in the context of wider consultation:

> Ofsted recognises the importance of listening to parents and carers, teachers and school leaders, and their unions; ...Historically, face to face meetings and

panels were mainly used to do this. However, social media, such as Twitter, has added another dimension to these opportunities to engage. It has widened the groups we speak to and while we recognise that the audience is self-selecting and not necessarily representative, it does link people very effectively and enables discussion about issues with immediacy that helps to break down barriers and bureaucracy. We recognise that this extra level of debate and discussion has had a positive impact on our practice.[12]

While Ofsted remains the area of reform where the influence of social media seems clearest, Sam Freedman suggests bloggers had influence on some other policies: "I can think of other examples – on GCSE/A-level reform and curriculum in particular – that led to small policy changes". In a blogpost, written after Gove's first speech mentioning bloggers, Freedman had claimed that blogs, while not being the driver of policy, were an essential corrective:

...Twitter and blogs are a lifeline; a way to access at least some unvarnished truth about what people really think. And while I don't want to overdo the impact of the blogosphere – policy is still primarily driven by the traditional internal processes – I do think its rise is having quite a profound effect.

Suddenly an insightful classroom teacher like Tessa Matthews[iii], Laura McInerney or Joe Kirby has a direct line of communication to the Secretary of State and his advisers. Anyone can make a case against a policy and if it's strong enough to be picked up and retweeted a few dozen times there's a good chance it will be read by the people who matter. I can think of a fair few changes to nascent policy ideas off the back of a particularly perceptive blogpost which raised points that had been missed during internal discussions...[13]

In addition to these insights claimed for engaging with social media, there has been some suggestion that bloggers affected the climate of ideas during this period. The article I referred to earlier by Bob Davis in the *Journal of Philosophy of Education* complained of current ideas 'permeating the educational blogosphere', where:

...a new style of knowledge production ...is at the present time, for example, seized by the intellectual fashion for the cognitive sciences (not, let it be stressed in their outdated and modish 'braingym'-type expressions, which are scorned) and for the incontestable credence these sciences apparently lend to a 'forms of knowledge' curriculum and an instructional teacher-centred pedagogy.[14]

The influence of certain ideas, common in blogs, is confirmed by Sam Freedman:

But perhaps more important [than changes to policy influenced by bloggers] were the ideas – [Daniel] Willingham, [Doug] Lemov etc. [two US educationalists who blogged and were widely cited by bloggers in the UK and whose ideas may well be argued to correspond to those described above] – that influenced the way Ministers thought about all issues and which is very evident from Gove speeches etc...

---

iii   A pseudonym for Katie Ashcroft

One former teacher blogger, Daisy Christodoulou, also recalls a change in the intellectual climate:

> In about 2009 or 2010, it felt much harder to talk about teaching knowledge, or about how the internet might not solve all of our problems. It felt as if there wasn't even a debate to be had about these issues – it was as though they had all been settled. The biggest change since then is that now, at least there is a debate. There are still plenty of people who disagree about the value of knowledge, but they can't just dismiss the opposite point of view. Similarly, there is much more evidence out there about the value of knowledge and about cognitive psychology, which it is hard for people just to ignore. So there is a new debate happening, and that is very exciting.

She adds:

> Social media gave a voice to teachers who disagreed with the mainstream views, helped them find other people who agreed with them, and made it easier for evidence and new ideas to be shared and publicised.

Of course, it is impossible to know to what extent this 'new debate' would have happened without social media. Debate, even involving those who write blogs or use twitter, is not limited to the online world. Many of those who were known as bloggers, are now better known for their wider involvement in education. Daisy Christodoulou is known as head of research at the Ark academy chain. Tom Bennett runs the organisation researchED. Robert Peal worked for the think tank Civitas. All three have written books about education. A number of bloggers, including many of those mentioned in this article now work in high profile free schools which often feature in the media. Many bloggers are no longer dependent on their blogs for their influence.[iv] Conversely, existing voices who were prominent in education, including academics, writers, and policy-makers have joined in with the use of social media.

That is not to say the influence of bloggers has affected all policy-makers, or been welcomed by everyone. The influence of teachers using social media, on Labour's education team has not been conspicuous. According to former editor of the Labour Teachers blog, John Blake:

> ...aside from the fact that Burnham, Twigg and Hunt all met with [Labour Teachers] and the last two came to our events, it is difficult to think of specific evidence of social media interaction...

> I can't think of any reason or evidence that would preclude a conclusion that Gove (not the Tories more generally who I think are much less engaged, as Morgan illustrates) was plugged very strongly into the educational social media world but that Labour was much slower to realise its power and slower again to engage.

Where there is criticism of the influence of bloggers, it has tended to claim they are

---

iv   In my opinion, the most plausible explanation why so many of the sources earlier referred to me personally is that I am one of the few bloggers who is still only known as a blogger.

the wrong people to listen to. The journal article by Bob Davis referred to 'blogocrats' and characterised bloggers as part of a long tradition of, 'carpet-baggers and gurus of various stripes hostile to mainstream educational thought and promising instant fixes for every educational or social ill' and criticised the injustice of their influence on policy. Davis considers those prominent on social media as powerful, misguided rivals to those already established in education circles.

Several of the leading commentators and critics who have emerged through these new media now command significant and energetic followings numerically much larger than the memberships of many learned societies or the subscribers to academic journals. Their timelines and followers, moreover, routinely include the officers of influential think tanks, spokesmen for ambitious publishers and policy-makers by no means passive in their association with the informing concepts and objectives. ... Michael Gove was shrewd enough to appreciate ... their register and their soundtrack as equally 'outsider' critics of the prevailing educational norms.[15]

The journalist and teacher, Francis Gilbert, who himself blogs, made similar comments in an article about the Headteacher and blogger Tom Sherrington:

Sherrington enjoys blogging and tweeting in his spare time; he doesn't see it as work. He's aware, though, that in recent years that a 'tweetocracy' amongst teachers has emerged; a number of tweeting and blogging teachers like him, many of them are listed on the homepage of his blog, have assumed dominance and power over the educational debate. This Tweetocracy get invited to all the prestigious educational events – conferences, launches, policy discussions etc – while others are left out. My worry here is that educational academics have become so marginalized[16].

To an extent, this may be considered part of a wider debate about whether politicians or educationalists should control the direction of education policy. Much criticism of politicians has been based on their supposed ignorance of, and remoteness from, the daily workings of the education system and the greater expertise of academics, officials and Headteachers who have worked in, or studied, education for a long time. Any narrative which contrasts the ignorance of politicians with the expertise of educationalists is undermined when there are voices from the frontline of the education system willing to comment on policy and willing to criticise educationalists and politicians alike for the impact their ideas have in the classroom. Simplistic assertions about ideological or pedagogical consensus amongst all those who work in education are no longer credible when hundreds or thousands of teachers are following individuals with contrasting views.

If teachers are in a position to evaluate what ideas are relevant to their practice, and share those evaluations with thousands of other teachers, then educationalists can no longer claim a monopoly over educational thought. Opinions that might be orthodoxy in academic journals, conventional wisdom among those training teachers or articles of faith held by like-minded professors of education, might be repeatedly revealed to be objects of derision among those who actually occupied classrooms. The most significant casualties of social media may turn out to be those who claimed expertise about the business of the classroom from positions which could not have been more insulated from the challenges and experiences of those actually in the classroom.

Other criticism of the influence of bloggers has questioned whether they provide a representative voice. After being amongst the first group of bloggers to visit Ofsted, Shena Lewington observed that:

> I am aware that one or two tweeters have questioned the make-up of the group ...and asked why there was not more representation from women, or from primary teachers, or non-Scots.

An article in *The Times* described the world of education blogging in this way:

> This world is ... rather male-dominated. Many of the most recognised education bloggers (the head teacher Geoff Barton, and the teachers Frank Chalk, Old Andrew and Tom Bennett, for example) are men.[17]

> "I try not to think about it as an old boys' network, but it's hard to escape the fact that it's quite hard to crack into the blogging establishment as a woman," says Bansi Kara, an English teacher who writes The New Stateswoman blog.

While the idea of a 'blogging establishment' which one has to 'crack' is somewhat fanciful[v], the idea that education bloggers are not representative of the wider population isn't.

Last December, with help from a large number of volunteers, I compiled a spreadsheet of information about all the education blogs written by people in, or from, the UK which I was aware of at that time.[18] Of those bloggers whose gender could be discerned (some writers were anonymous; some blogs were written by more than one writer), 514 were male and 319 were female. This 62% to 38% split contrasts with a school workforce (using figures for England alone in 2013) which is 80% female and a teaching profession which is 74% female.[19] While the sector in which education bloggers worked was not identified in a large minority of cases, of those blogs where it was, there were almost twice as many education bloggers working in the secondary sector as the primary sector, despite there being little difference in the size of the two teaching workforces. Of 642 education bloggers whose position was identified, there were 339 who were identified simply as a 'teacher', 80 as 'SLT' and 39 as a 'Headteacher'. The other large group represented among education bloggers were 75 consultants.

It would seem that the population of education bloggers is noticeably skewed towards men and towards secondary teachers and while, to my knowledge, no figures exist on the number of education consultants, they do seem particularly well

---

v   My own experience, after eight and a half years of blogging and reading blogs is that longevity and frequency of posting are the main qualifications needed to be recognised as a successful or important blogger.

represented. Anyone hoping to discern the general balance of opinions among those working in education, or among teachers from education blogs alone is likely to be working with a noticeably unrepresentative sample. However, what does seem to be the case is that education blogs do provide access to the opinions of hundreds of teachers and dozens of Heads which simply wasn't available before. Whether those setting the direction within the education system make use of this will no doubt depend on how they value this access. Some who are, or have played important roles in the education system do value being able to find quickly the opinions of some of those who are currently teaching. Amanda Spielman, the chair of exams regulator Ofqual, claimed social media provided 'the kind of feedback that all public bodies need' in a form which was easily shared. She listed a number of ways this feedback was useful:

- they capture intelligent voices direct from the school/classroom, particularly valuable when what actually happens in the classroom is little understood elsewhere
- they provide near-instant response (Twitter) and speedy response (blogs)
- the quality of comment and analysis is generally high, sometimes exceptionally so
- it is clearly easier for teachers to break with consensus on social media than in a staff room, so there is more real debate
- the cover of anonymity can help to air things that have been essentially unmentionable
- they provide a regular reminder that those on the receiving end of policy and regulation can have perceptions that are a long way adrift from actual intentions, and that addressing these perceptions is often just as important as addressing substantive issues

Dominic Cummings also sees lessons to be learnt from social media:

What needs to happen is the policy system really becomes systematically adaptive to what is happening on the ground but of course very few people with power have an incentive to make this happen and it is inherently hard given the hard wiring of contemporary Whitehall.

Debate over education is not new, and the growth of social media is not the cause of that debate, a reliable indicator of its extent, nor its only expression. However, it does enable an increasingly diverse range of teachers to engage with debate about education policy, and policy-makers to debate and engage with teachers.

When I began blogging, I was frequently told that nobody else thought what I did. There was no debate to be had about problems with behaviour in our schools. There was no dissent to the proposition that children learnt best in groups, or the idea that skills were more important than knowledge. There was no reason to think that exams had become easier, or that the curriculum had been reduced in rigour. Even common experiences of teachers, like boring INSET or unsupportive managers, were dismissed as being either my invention; my fault, or down to my being overly influenced by experience in one school.

As more teachers joined Twitter or wrote blogs, and more voices from the classroom challenged the orthodoxies of the day I found that those who wished to silence me could no longer deny that there were more like me out there. Those who once told me that I should be quiet because everybody knew I was wrong, moved to accusing me of causing trouble by encouraging a small number of like-minded individuals. Eventually they began saying that I should be quiet because nobody really disagreed with the content of what I was saying or that people might be too intimidated to disagree with me.

The old consensus in education no longer exists on social media. While this may not be true of other parts of the education world, anyone in education policy-making, or teaching, who wants to experience the debate and hear the diversity of opinions, can easily find challenges to every orthodoxy online.

### Endnotes

1   The full list can be found in the sidebar, under the heading "Blogs from March 2015" on educationechochamberuncut.wordpress.com/ [accessed March, 2015].

2   Davis, B. (2014) 'Editorial' *Journal of Philosophy of Education*, Vol. 48, No. 3.

3   www.publications.parliament.uk/pa/cm200506/cmhansrd/vo061023/debtext/61023-0002.htm [accessed March, 2015]; news.bbc.co.uk/1/hi/programmes/panorama/7002977.stm [accessed March, 2015].

4   All quotations which are provided without an individual reference are from personal correspondence undertaken for the purpose of writing this article.

5   Gove, M. 'Speech to teachers and headteachers', speech to National College for Teaching and Leadership on 25 April 2013.

6   At a debate at the LSE he made a reference to Tom Bennett and I www.lse.ac.uk/newsAndMedia/videoAndAudio/channels/publicLecturesAndEvents/player.aspx?id=1906 [accessed March, 2015]; Gove, M. 'What does it mean to be an educated person?', speech to Brighton College on 9 May 2013; Gove, M. 'The Importance of Teaching', speech to Policy Exchange on 5 September 2013; In a podcast he mentioned John Blake and I blogs.telegraph.co.uk/news/telegram/100258501/good-nick-and-wicked-nick-michael-gove-teases-clegg-over-pandering-to-left-wing-activists/ [accessed March, 2015].

7   www.publications.parliament.uk/pa/cm201314/cmselect/cmeduc/c65-i/c6501.htm [accessed March, 2015].

8   pragmaticreform.wordpress.com/2014/08/02/bloggers-reform-ofsted/ [accessed March, 2015].

9   Gove, M. 'The Importance of Teaching', speech to Policy Exchange on 5 September 2013.

10   Griffiths, S. 'Schools watchdog at war with Gove', *The Sunday Times*, 26 January 2014.

11   www.learningspy.co.uk/featured/ofsteds-new-inspection-handbook-cause-celebration/ [accessed March, 2015].

12   www.workingoutwhatworks.com/en-GB/Resource-library/Videos/2014/rED-v-Ofsted-2014 [accessed March, 2015].

13   samfreedman1.blogspot.co.uk/2013/04/the-internet-is-flat.html [accessed March, 2015]

14  Davis, B (2014).

15  Ibid.

16  www.localschoolsnetwork.org.uk/2014/12/the-tweeting-headteacher-who-took-over-the-world/ [accessed March, 2015].

17  Ebner, S. 'An old boy's network', *The Times*, 8 November 2012.

18  docs.google.com/spreadsheets/d/142e0Wpri8ZhzmQXqImNjQA2dI_JnaB9PvIDgt8lGHVs/edit#gid=2133650911 [accessed March, 2015].

19  www.gov.uk/government/uploads/system/uploads/attachment_data/file/335413/sfr11_2014_updated_july.pdf [accessed March, 2015].

# Policy: Ten challenges for any government from 2015

## Jonathan Simons

Almost nothing has been left untouched in education policy over the past five years. This has been fascinating, and the public and education profession have been blessed (I mean this seriously) to have heavyweight politicians from all parties holding the education brief. When politicians stop taking education seriously, children lose out.

Over the past decade I have witnessed education reform first hand: as a civil servant in HM Treasury, the Cabinet Office and No 10; in a senior strategy role for Serco within the education practice which held outsourced contracts across a range of areas; and now as Head of Education at the think tank Policy Exchange. But one of the weaknesses of the education discourse over that time has been that there has been almost no discussion of some of the underlying principles of reform espoused by government or opposition. Nor has there been any sustained engagement with the perpetual knotty challenges with the English system which hamper policy effectiveness. This chapter attempts to begin the process of unpicking ten of the most significant challenges in education policy which will afflict any future government.

These are less specific policy problems, though some of them have specific policy solutions. They are more themes and weaknesses in the way in which the English school system thinks and operates that need to be addressed if we are to make a step change in the overall system performance. The challenges are presented as a starter for further discussion rather than a definitive list, and they draw on concrete examples from the 2010-2015 Parliament.

In no particular order, I think the ten challenges for future school reform from 2015 are these:

**1. An unresolved question, driven by values above evidence, about schools' role in addressing wider social issues**. Over the past 50 or so years, the academic debate around what is termed school effectiveness has veered (and I paraphrase) between those who thought that structures of society were so strong that schools could do little or nothing to compensate for that,[1] and that at the other extreme schools can (and should) act to close or eliminate the social inequities which lead to academic inequality within their own pupils, and hence close the attainment gap.[2]

This is not the place to attempt to summarise the research on both sides, nor to provide my own non-expert view. But the often heated nature of this debate speaks to a wider issue which affects the development of English education policy around values. The question is less whether schools *can* compensate for the differences which emerge (and are reinforced) outside their gates, but whether they *ought* to be charged with doing this – and if so, how much, and by what mechanism? Almost all national policy-making flows from an implicit or explicit answer to this question. Perhaps paradoxically, those who tend to argue that schools can have limited impact are keener on giving schools greater responsibility for trying to address them – consider, for example, the extensive work under the Labour government between 2007-2010, especially with the creation of the Department for Children, Schools and Families and the publication of the Children's Plan.[3] By contrast, the 2010-2015 coalition government was explicit from Day 1 that it saw schools' core purposes as being to teach, hence the totemic return to the name 'the Department for Education' (which it had not been since 1995) and the abolition of almost all of the Children's Plan's requirements.[i]

But the nature of this debate of values means that it cannot be solved by evidence. There is no academic paper in the school effectiveness field which will convince either side on how best to address a large correlation in England between socio-economic status and achievement. There is no school that can demonstrate a weakening of the link through a stronger academic focus, nor any example of outstanding partnership work doing the same, that will achieve consensus. Nor can it be solved by branding it a false dichotomy. It is a clash of values, and it drives and will continue to drive policy and funding allocations (both within and outside the schools budget).

2. **A school system that is both centralised and localised at once**. Tim Brighouse has said that: "Before 1980 the state had three powers over the schooling system; approval of the removal of air-raid shelters from school grounds, decisions on how many teachers could be trained each year, and decide the size of the building programmes that LEAs should use to build sufficient school places." Following the Education Act 2011, the Secretary of State now has, by Brighouse's estimate, over 2,000 powers.[4] This stands in stark contrast to the rhetoric of almost all government policy since 2010, which has been about granting powers to schools. But it is not just rhetoric – the OECD considers that schools in England have amongst the greatest freedom of any member country, combining autonomy over allocating resources with autonomy in making decisions about curriculum and assessment.[5] Local Authorities sit uncomfortably in the middle, increasingly hollowed out over the past 25 years, but still holding responsibility for discharging 198 statutory functions in the fields of education and children's services as of March 2013.[6]

How can England have both a centralised *and* an autonomous system? Partly, it depends what is means by autonomy – schools can in theory have autonomy from a National Curriculum, but if all their students enter the same public exams and follow the same exam board syllabuses, such autonomy is in practice quite limited. But partly this tension it reflects a deep-seated belief in decentralisation from central government, combined with a (justified) nervousness that variation in performance will be punished and the impact will be felt centrally. Hence what can seem an endless back and forth.

---

i   See for example the speech by Nick Gibb to annual conference of ATL: "My view is that the best way for schools to tackle social problems … is to make sure children leave school well-educated. That is the best way out of poverty." As reported in *The Guardian*, 3 April 2012.

To give some examples from 2010-2015:

| Decentralising / autonomous measures | Centralising / prescriptive measures |
|---|---|
| A new, slimmed National Curriculum for primaries | Mandatory phonics teaching in all primaries |
| A substantially reduced Ofsted framework | Some new things being put back into that framework – eg Fundamental British Values |
| Disapplication of the entire National Curriculum for thousands of secondary (and primary) academies | The introduction of the EBacc as a soft performance measurement at secondary |
| A freeing up of the pay and conditions framework for teachers | The requirement for all maintained schools to introduce Performance Related Pay |
| The decentralisation of support for disadvantaged students via the Pupil Premium | Requiring detailed reporting on the impact and spending of that same pupil premium |
| The abolition of levels for measuring pupil progress | A new baseline test for measuring progress across primary schools |

This tension flows from a lack of a clear spatial dimension towards education policy, from lack of system leaders, and from no consensus on the role of politicians (all issues I will go on to discuss). It also contributes to reform fatigue.

**3. Reform fatigue**. Unquestionably, the past five years (but really ever since 1997) have been a whirlwind of change in which almost no element of the school system has remain untouched. My personal view is that pace, in general, is a positive thing when trying to enact change within a system, particularly one with some of the issues England faces (of which more below), but when combined with rhetoric and policy to grant schools more autonomy, contributes to the confusion between central and local. In addition, and as a consequence, the system becomes increasingly unwilling to engage in further reforms, and diminishing marginal returns kick in as they are adopted with less enthusiasm, or consciously or subconsciously ignored or delayed due to the perception that they will all change again soon anyway.

I should stress at this point that this is not a defining argument for 'letting teachers get on with it', or arbitrarily setting rules on how long policies have to run for before they can be reformed, although there may be good reasons in practice for following one or both of these maxims in specific instances. Nor is it an argument for 'taking politics out of education' – reform fatigue can and does exist outside of political whim (even in a school led system, individual leaders may decide to enact change in their school or groups of schools and have to address reform fatigue). But unquestionably in 2015, any government will face the twin issues of changes still needing to be made, and a school system largely reluctant at having to do it.

**4. A shortage of leaders**. Twenty-one per cent of primary Headteachers and 29% of secondary Headteachers are approaching retirement within in the next ten years and there are, especially at primary level, insufficient people ready and willing to step up and replace them.[7] More broadly, there are insufficient leaders, not just Heads or SLT but middle leaders as well, ready and willing to work in the schools that most desperately need the support and consistency which they can bring. None of this is to denigrate the people currently doing it, to ignore the deterrents in the system towards taking on Headship in particular, or to attack the schemes that attempted between 2010 and 2015 to address this (Talented Leaders, National Teaching Service, Future Leaders *et al*). But the fact remains that a self-improving school system needs a fully stacked team of leaders and real bench depth – and currently we don't have either.

A lack of leaders also contributes to the important issue of a lack of capacity building in the English system. It isn't enough to have freedoms if the system is not equipped to step up and make use of them. As we wrote in the foreword to our Policy Exchange manifesto:

> Whilst freedom is a necessary component of an autonomous system, it is not sufficient to sustain it. The fight for freedom, waged successfully over successive governments, must now give way to the next stage – to empower leaders in education to make use of their freedoms as they see fit.[8]

Absent a sufficient number of people to take on leadership positions in schools, and in particular a sufficient number of what are sometimes termed system leaders (people willing and able to have an effect and lead across more than one institution) any policy pronouncement will be severely curtailed.

**5. No clear spatial approach to school reform**. England, like many highly developed countries, has a highly concentrated population in a small proportion of space. Around 65% of the population live in highly dense urban areas, and about 35% of the population live in major cities. But those 65% people only live in 15% of England's land space, which means we also have about a third of the population scattered around 85% of our territory. Some high performing educational countries are marked by dense urban populations (much of East Asia), and some have disparate populations over large geographies (Canada). But few have both. In fact, looking at the top ten countries in PISA, perhaps only New Zealand has a similar demographic mix as England, and with a far smaller population overall.

The significance of this unusual split, when combined with a relatively large population, is that England can neither have an education system which is very centralised, nor one which is very distributed. We have too big a population of teachers to centrally move around individuals in the way that Shanghai does, for example. We cannot afford to focus solely on cities to raise standards, but nor can we design everything on a model for smaller provinces and rural areas. There is no natural regional level in England (something which affects not just education). The dominant thesis in English reform for addressing this over the past twenty years or so, including from 2010, has been to largely ignore geography except at a macro level. So we have City Challenges, and we have a small school subsidy in the funding system. We talk – without acting much – on the specific challenges of coastal towns and coalfield areas. But I can't think of any serious focus and analysis in recent years on why *one city* has done better than *another city* (outside of recent focus on the specific London effect), or why certain rural areas are bucking the trends that hold their peers back. Issues are considered either in aggregate (how can we improve coastal towns regardless of where they are, or how can we raise the performance of white working class boys regardless of whether they come from ex-industrial towns or rural areas) or at micro-school level (how can all schools be like school x).

**6. The 'learned helplessness' of too much of the profession**. As noted above, OECD comparisons tell us that school leaders in England have probably the greatest level of school autonomy in the world. Similarly, at an individual classroom level, teachers are in theory the masters of their domain. Unlike many other countries, we do not have state approved textbooks, many schools do not (need to) follow a National Curriculum, we have competing syllabi for exams with a wide range of content to choose from, and lessons are structured for varying amount of times. Yet in practice, many teachers (and Heads) will say they have no autonomy at all: citing variously SLT prescription, Ofsted, national exams, and league tables and the accountability system overall.

Although such facets of the system undeniably can hamper flexibility, the issue is often also one of 'learned helplessness' – an inability or unwillingness to break out of a destructive pattern of simply awaiting direction from above. Too many schools and teachers, who have served their professional career in a system that has previously been (and in some ways still is) so top down, now seem unwilling to grasp the opportunities offered to them. The net effect of this is that whilst the current government has made a genuine and concerted effort to strip back regulation and grant more autonomy to teachers, such efforts have been almost entirely in vain. Despite regular and justifiable demands that government 'treat teaching as a profession', with clear evidence of areas where government ought not to mandate, there are too often moves from the profession in the opposite direction. Whether it is the abolition of levels, greater flexibility over how teachers can be trained, or greater options over delivery of careers advice, the counter-intuitive plea from teachers and learned third parties has often been for more prescription, or at a minimum for more strong guidance as to the 'right' way to do something. This cycle needs to be broken. Both the recent ASCL blueprint – which rightly and self consciously sets out more asks for Headteachers than for government – and the moves towards a College of Teaching are positive indications, but much more remains to be done.

**7. A need to evolve the theory of school improvement**. Ever since the 1980s, across much of the Western world (or at least the Anglosphere), public services have been overseen via a theory known as New Public Management (NPM). This broadly holds that market style management of public services is the most efficient way of raising standards; whilst recognising the unique features of public services compared to private service. Reformers who are influenced by NPM have introduced to public services features based on the belief that certain features of a market system – such as choice and competition, diverse operators, measurable metrics and objectives and clear incentives – can effectively increase performance in a public service. In education, this manifests itself through clear headline metrics for measuring school performance (*ie* 5

A\*-C published in league tables); the operation of school choice/parental preferences; schools being governed by a range of groups not just government; a process to allow good schools to expand and less popular ones to close; money following the pupils and so on. There is not space here to debate whether such a philosophy has worked – from a personal perspective, I am a strong advocate for it and believe it has contributed hugely to a rising of standards in schools since the Education Reform Act of 1988, under governments of both stripes.[ii] But as thinkers and policy experts in education such as Chris Cook and Sir Michael Barber have postulated, we may be coming towards a period in which it offers diminishing returns.[9]

NPM has achieved close to total intellectual dominance amongst public policy officials and policymakers (including politicians). This is not to say, however, that the general approach categorised as NPM, or sometimes more witheringly as 'neo liberal reform' or even 'GERM' (the Global Education Reform Movement), has not evolved. One can chart significant differences in approach and belief to education reforms from the approach taken by the Conservatives in the 1980s, to the early Blair government reforms, to the latter Blair reforms and the approach taken by the coalition. Indeed, as I have written elsewhere, one of Gove's legacies is shifting the internal legitimate frame for policy debate in education within Conservative circles.[10]

But the fact remains that for some, adherence not just to the general approach of NPM but to all of its consequences remains an article of faith. It has also been all too easy for defenders of an NPM approach to paint all objections as 'soft on standards' and avoid serious scrutiny in that way. It should be incumbent on such defenders, and again I freely class myself as one, not to be satisfied with having achieved intellectual dominance and to have been vindicated by an overall rise in standards. We should also accept the weaknesses of such a system – for example in the limiting nature of elements of the accountability system, and take on the responsibility to evolve this thinking.

**8. A lack of mechanisms for spreading innovation.** A well-worn question across the public sector is why innovation doesn't flourish and best practice doesn't scale. There is significant variation between schools in their effectiveness at securing outcomes for their students, even amongst schools serving similar populations. Such variance is even bigger within a school.[11] Other UK evidence from the early 2000s suggested that the UK specific within school variance could be much higher. A DfE funded study of 2003 data showed that 'in value-added terms, key stage 2 (KS2) within-school variation is five times greater than between school variance, for KS3 it's 11 times greater and for KS4 it's 14 times greater'.[12] So in other words, good practice being demonstrated by a teacher on the same corridor often isn't being shared, let alone good practice from a school down the road or on the other side of the country. Many attempts have been made to synthesise this issue from an academic perspective.[13]

---

ii   This is testified to by headline indicators of exam passes, indicators as to children's wider outcomes, proxy measures such as the number and quality of graduates wanting to become teachers, and simply a general consensus amongst the profession as to the quality of school standards compared to 20 or even 10 years ago.

A recent Cabinet Office literature review identifies eight key factors for successfully spreading innovation,[14] of which in my estimation, despite noble exceptions, the school system scores, at best, 2.5.[iii]

Breaking this down, it is clear that there are a number of factors which hamper systemic innovation spreading in the school system. These include incentives not to spread innovation, such as a risk aversion as to whether innovation would hamper a school's performance in the short term, or the way in which schools can see themselves as competing directly with their peers for relative and absolute position or limited resources (pupils, staff), as well as practical barriers to address small but real life barriers such as teachers teaching every day and having limited time to speak to each other or observe each other, or money available to copy and share learning resources. It also includes the absence of incentives to spread innovation. For a school with consistent results well above floor target, and an 'outstanding' Ofsted rating, what direct incentives are there to continue to improve? As Mulgan and Albury point out, the profit motive would be the normal driver in many 'markets', which does not exist here.[iv] Of course moral purpose, mission and a sense of communal spirit is an incentive for some, including many teachers sharing resources for free via *TES*. So is personal status for some high-flying school leaders. But these may well not drive all decision-makers. Moreover, until recently, there has been little mechanism for sharing innovation – although developments such as School Direct, academy chains, Teaching Schools, and grass roots discussions of research via social media all offer opportunities for addressing that.

**9. No consensus on the role of politics and elected politicians**. The common call at present is to 'take education out of politics' – whether this relates to the curriculum, teaching standards, assessment or other school related activities. In the run up to the 2015 election, this was rejected by Nicky Morgan from the Conservatives, and Tristram Hunt from Labour has stayed silent on the issue.[15] David Laws for the Liberal Democrats has suggested a greater role for expert groups in making judgements on some issues.[16] My own personal perspective is that this would be a mistake. Education is an essentially personal and political issue in which the democratic representative of the electorate must be allowed to make decisions. The solution to constant changes, which is undoubtedly an issue, is not the construction of a bureaucratic edifice, but a self-denying ordinance from politicians. Hunt in particular recognised this, being

---

iii  The eight elements, with my assessment of the school system's position against them, are 'build a culture that rewards and encourages scaling up innovation' (no), 'make the business case and demonstrate the social return' (no), 'embed skills needed for scaling up and understand that skills to innovate and to scale up are different' (no), 'develop and use networks to make connections, provide advice, share knowledge and create dialogue' (half), 'embed processes and mechanisms that facilitate scaling up' (no), 'recognise that a feeling of ownership acts as an incentive to share learning about what works' (yes), 'manage resources, funding, expertise and support to actively encourage scaling up.' (no) and 'credibility, endorsement and reputation provide the business case for scaling up' (yes).

iv  To avoid the risk of being misunderstood, I should make clear that I don't think there should be a profit motive in mainstream education.

very clear that on issues such as the key stage 4 curriculum, he might not like it but he had pledged to maintain it.[17]

But the reason that this is a system challenge is that, in truth, the position of many people with regard to politics and politicians is schizophrenic. All too often, when people argue for taking politics out of education or creating an expert council, they mean implicitly 'so that more people like me can have a say'. Many of the same people (broadly defined as on the left) who argue for the Secretary of State to stay out of politics also mourn the lack of democratic oversight with the withering away of the local authority. Similarly, many people (broadly defined as on the right) who defend the Secretary of State's powers are also nervous about, say, having binding parental ballots on academy conversions. It is one of those irregular political verbs – I *am carrying out the wishes of my electorate*, you *are ignoring the evidence*, he *is an ideologue.* This is not an education specific issue – within the health service, for example, often cited by those in education as a best practice comparator, there was uproar during the passing of the Health and Social Care Act about whether the Secretary of State would or would not retain in statue the duty 'to provide or secure the provision of health services' (as opposed to delegating it to an, er, expert council called NHS England).[18] This lack of a consensus over what politics should and should not do – including the option of agreeing it remain arbitrary – needs to be resolved.

**10. A default strategy of improvement via the raising of minimum standards.** The focus of government policy for a number of years across all parties has been to raise standards and narrow the gap. It has largely done so through a focus on raising the performance at the bottom end through increasingly stretching floor targets and with an accountability system for individual schools which requires them to exceed such targets. As an alternative it would be entirely possible to design a system strategy which sought above all else to raise the performance at the top end, even at the theoretical cost of widening the gap between the top performers and the bottom performers. As Andreas Schleicher regularly points out, one can also achieve – as some countries in PISA have – a system in which the average standard is high, the top performers are world beating, and the system is broadly equitable.

> The rhetoric of government and associated bodies since 2010 has paid heed to the need to move beyond simply raising the performance at the lower end. There is much talk of making the final shift from Good to Great, or recognising that, to quote the American schools reformer Joel Klein, "We can mandate adequacy but must unleash greatness". Yet the fact remains that almost all government actions from 2010 have been to continue to focus on raising standards at the bottom. It is worth emphasising that there may well be sound reasons to adopt such an approach – given that what marks the UK out internationally is less its overall performance or even its percentage of high achievers but instead its relatively long tail of low skilled individuals both within schools and post education. My concern is that the trade-offs between such strategies are rarely ever debated.
>
> We need to have an open discussion about which strategy our system takes from 2015 onwards. This has consequences not just for the accountability system

but many other policy levers including curriculum, teacher training, and system oversight and inspection.

The ten challenges set out here are unquestionably complex to address. Many of them, as noted throughout the text, are interrelated. And to top it all off, they are not easily amenable to single policy interventions. However, this is not a counsel of despair. Simply raising awareness of these questions and debating them increases the likelihood of finding answers: for if a school led system means anything, it must means solutions emerging from collective discussion rather than from Whitehall.

## Endnotes

1   Most famously in Bernstein, B. 'Education cannot compensate for society', *New Society*, 26th February 1970.

2   The academic debate is neatly summarised in Reynolds, D., Chapman, C., Kelly, A., Mujis, D. and Sammons, P. 'Educational effectiveness: the development of the discipline, the critiques, the defence, and the present debate' *Effective Education*, Vol 3 No 2, September 2012.

3   Department for Children, Schools and Families, *The Children's Plan*, December 2007. The foreword by Ed Balls is explicit about the values that underpin the document: "The Plan and the new Department mean that more than ever before families will be at the centre of excellent, integrated services that put their needs first, regardless of traditional institutional and professional structures. This means a new leadership role for Children's Trusts in every area, a new role for schools as the centre of their communities, and more effective links between schools, the NHS and other children's services so that together they can engage parents and tackle all the barriers to the learning, health and happiness of every child."

4   Brighouse, T., 'The tyranny of an over mighty state', speech to the Sunday Times Festival of Education at Wellington College on 21 June 2012.

5   OECD (2011) *PISA in focus No 9: School autonomy and accountability: are they related to student performance*.

6   Policy Exchange (2014), *Primary Focus: the next stage of improvement for primary schools in England*.

7   Ibid.

8   Policy Exchange (2015), *Education Manifesto*.

9   Cook, C. 'Risks of government schools strategy', *BBC News*, 2 February 2015; and Barber, M. (2014) *Preparing for a Renaissance in Assessment*, Pearson.

10  Simons, J. 'The Gove legacy and the politics of education after 2015' in Finn, M. (2015) *The Gove Legacy: Education in Britain After the Coalition*, Palgrave Pivot.

11  OECD, 'PISA 2009 Results: Learning trends change in student performance since 2000', 2009.

12  Hopkins, D., Reynolds, D. and Gray, J. (2005) *School improvement: lessons from research*, DfES.

13  Mulgan, G. and Albury, D. (2003) *Innovation in the Public Sector*, Strategy Unit.

14  Capability Building Programme Project Group (2011) *Scaling Up Innovation in the Public Sector*, National School of Government.

15  Coughlan, S. 'Morgan rejects heads' independent curriculum body', *BBC News*, 21 March 2015.

16  Liberal Democrats (2014) *Pre manifesto 2014: A stronger economy and a fairer society*, p. 43.

17  'Labour says it will keep Gove school reforms', *BBC News*, 2 March 2014.

18  See for example the legal opinion commissioned by the pressure group 38 Degrees, here www.38degrees.org.uk/page/content/NHS-legal-advice/ [accessed March 2015]

# Teaching: Teacher professionalism, training and autonomy

## Tom Bennett

Is teaching actually a profession? Many would insist that it is, but perhaps, as John David Blake put it, it is an immature profession.[1] This is because when we look to other paradigms of that word, such a law, accountancy or medicine, it would be tempting to see several features in common:

1. A body of established knowledge and wisdom.

2. Certification processes that are commonly agreed and lead to incrementally senior progression.

3. Autonomy of action within prescribed limits, within which the authority of the professional is recognised as paramount, and trusted.

However, any one of these features could be challenged in relation to the teaching profession: the body of knowledge in teaching is often a battlefield of biases and ideologies from all angles; training programs are disputed; and autonomy of action is so restricted as to be vanishingly small.

It would be fatuous to say that autonomy is intrinsically valuable – few abstracts are. But the contemporary UK teacher could be excused for feeling their job is characterised by prescription rather than permissiveness. Issues surrounding curriculum, training, workload, accountability and performance management all conspire to circumscribe the teacher role in many ways. To understand how this situation came about, it is necessary to analyse several factors: how teachers are trained; their level of autonomy at any level of decision-making; and how their training is consolidated and reinforced throughout their careers.

### Building a teacher: training

The process of how we build teachers is a relatively modern question. Prior to the 20th century it was uncommon for teachers to be trained specifically as teachers at all. Subject knowledge or character were far more common interview shibboleths. The advent of universal state education, and the need to mass produce professionals who could cope with this process, led to the institution of teacher training in the UK.

Until recently, teacher training in the UK was a relatively uncomplicated process. Every teacher in the state sector had to have Qualified Teacher Status (QTS). In order to achieve this they had to go through Initial Teacher Training (ITT) which could be obtained through an undergraduate degree route, or a post graduate route, usually shorter. Entrants needed a degree or equivalent to at least 2:2 level, plus possess a C pass (or equivalent) in English and maths. If you already had a degree, you could enter the profession through the Graduate Teacher Program (GTP), working in a school as you train. Or you could train through School Centred Initial Teacher Training (SCITT). However, the Post Graduate Certificate in Education (PGCE) was the dominant route for postgraduate teachers, where candidates split a year between teaching in placement schools, and university based instruction.

In 2012 the Secretary of State for Education, Michael Gove, rolled his brisk reform programme into the teacher training sector. The schools-based training was to receive much more funding – in September 2013 a quarter of funding shifted from universities to schools, sending shockwaves through that sector, as schemes like School Direct were created and rolled out. Predictably this caused problems with shortages; with less control from the centre about how and where teachers would be trained, some areas – such as maths and science – saw deficits. One criticism came from the universities themselves, which believed that the changes had happened too broadly and quickly. James Noble-Rogers, of the Universities Council for the Education of Teachers, said introducing the scheme could "destabilise existing teacher education programmes to such an extent a lot of them will be at risk of closure".[2]

Russell Hobby, of the National Association of Head Teachers, said: "This is an area where 'the market' will not provide the best solutions. Schools need clarity and certainty if they are to make the significant commitment of looking after a trainee."[3]

In addition, Gove announced an expansion of the Teach First program. Teach First was a charity aimed at recruiting high-achieving graduates and training them in some of the most disadvantaged schools in the UK. It is two-year programme, with substantial off site support, where the bulk of the teacher experience comes from learning as you work.

In a speech to the National College in 2012, Gove's rebuff to the institutions of university-based teacher training could not have been clearer:

> The idea is a simple one: take the very best schools, ones that are already working to improve other schools, and put them in charge of teacher training and professional development for the whole system.[4]

In 2011 the government announced that it would accept – but no longer fund – applicants with less than a second class degree in their subject. Gove also oversaw the creation of Teaching Schools – clearly modelled on teaching hospitals as centres of excellence with the honour and responsibility of training future generations of teachers.

Other, more boutique routes into teaching are now possible. Apart from the relatively well-known Teach First avenue is the much smaller Troops To Teachers programs which aims to relocate suitably qualified candidates from the military into teaching roles, and Researchers into Schools, aimed at researchers who have finished, or nearly finished their doctorate, and want to develop a dual role both in and out of schools. The undergraduate path still exists, and thrives.

In the academic year 2014/15, the following numbers of teachers progressing through each path were as follows:[5]

| Route | Trainees recruited |
|---|---|
| **All Routes** | **32,543** |
| **Main Routes** | |
| Post-graduate (total) | 26,218 |
| Provider-led<br>School Direct (unsalaried)<br>School Direct (salaried) | 16,986<br>6,451<br>2,781 |
| Undergraduate (total) | 5,938 |
| **Additional Routes** | |
| Teach First | 1,387 |
| Troops to Teachers | 93 |

How effective has teacher training in the UK been? It depends on your milestone. According to data from the DfE, 9% of teachers leave the profession within the first year, which is a high rate of attrition; some have claimed it indicates equally high levels of unpreparedness for a profession that is, by anyone's estimate, an emotionally, intellectually and often physically demanding one.[6]

In 2014 Andrew Carter was installed as the chair of a panel tasked by the Secretary of State for Education to investigate the health of the ITT program in England and Wales. The following year, Carter delivered a diplomatic but definite verdict; not quite a rebuke, but certainly a clear message that ITT needed significant revitalisation.

## Autonomy

Teaching, despite its essentially social basis, can often seem a lonely vocation: the classroom teacher is frequently the only adult in the room, and it is very easy for a teacher to spend the majority of his or her professional life free from physical observation by other professionals. Many teachers comment that, after their initial training year(s) where scrutiny is often constant, succeeding years are solitary.

On the face of it, this context could be ripe for the development of extraordinary levels of independence. The reverse is true.

One reason is the advent of the National Curriculum. Prior to the 1988 Education Act, schools were under no prescription to teach specific syllabus content, although broad requirements were in place to prevent wanton individualism. Prescription was reserved for the later, examinable stages of the student's career. The advent of the National Curriculum created a systematised curricular skeleton that no school in the maintained sector could afford to ignore. The stated aims of this project were, as usual, to insist on floor standards, but it was also a project focused on standardisation.

Curriculums are set, in the most part by exam boards under direction from Ofqual, itself under direction from the DfE. Teachers may be involved as part of broader consultative processes, but they have no formal authority over the process. Exam board curriculums theoretically have scope for choice within their offers: texts, topics and so on. Within these spaces, teachers have some air to breath and room to move, selecting courses that match their skill base and familiarity. Practically, however, further obstacles to autonomy exist: school texts are infrequently replaced due to budgetary considerations, and often decisions about what to teach can be made for reasons other than subject specific ones. For example, it was notable that many English departments chose to study *Of Mice and Men* because of its shorter length relative to other novels on the same syllabus. Recent controversies about grade inflation have revealed that exam boards, through a system designed to encourage competition, were incrementally less challenging as years progressed. Within the RE community, for example, one exam board was famously more lenient/ easier than the rest.

So exceeding what is taught is rarely within the grasp of most teachers; simply delivering the prescribed content is more than enough.

## Teaching methods

On the surface, this should be an area where the teacher practitioner enjoys the most autonomy. How a class is taught, if not what, must surely be within the grasp of any one in charge of a classroom. But no, circumstances have conspired to deny even this to the modern teacher. Pedagogy has been dominated by a number of important levers which have meant that teachers have quite extraordinary pressure on their method and style.

Of these, Ofsted's influence cannot be overestimated or overstated. The inspection body, which arbitrates over the continued existence of schools, is the most powerful lever in education, beyond funding agreements. To receive a poor grade from Ofsted is to lead to the edge of a precipice that easily terminates with a school's closure, the Head's removal, or forced academisation. In short, Oftsed inspections have become the ultimate terminal exam. Head teachers are under enormous pressure to meet its expectations, which means teachers are too.

One of the least attractive features of recent years has been the growth of a cargo cult surrounding Ofsted, where schools seize every published expectation of the inspection body, and attempt to work out what 'Oftsed are looking for.' Given that their published expectations are clear in the abstract but short on detail, this has led schools to second guessing the inspectors, extrapolating wildly. Many schools have wrongly taken Ofsted guidelines on teaching and learning, and created their own laboratory lesson observation templates, despite the fact that Ofsted have never published such a thing.

This reduces lessons to a checklist; a series of observable metrics that can be extracted and isolated in brief snapshots of a lesson. So, it becomes possible for a teacher to be judged unsatisfactory because feature 'x' wasn't found, for example, group work or project work, depending on the inspector's belief about what constitutes a good lesson. The complex enterprise of teaching is reduced to a serious of ticks and shibboleths.

A preferred style of teaching was long denied by Ofsted, until it became irrefutably evident through inspector feedback that in fact, certain things were indeed being looked for: most notably strategies such as group work, discovery learning, independent work, and less teacher talk. It became so obvious that this had become a problem that the Chief Inspector of Ofsted, Sir Michael Wilshaw, was moved to declare publicly that from now inspectors were not to prefer any such strategies, instead focussing on learning outcomes rather than processes.[7] However at the time of writing it remains to be seen if this has filtered down the trunk into the branches, or whether or not inspectors now simply replicate earlier judgements but fail to mention the reasons.

Finally, a significant obstacle to teacher autonomy is the process by which they continue their training beyond the ITT stage. Continuing professional development (CPD) currently has little regulation; schools are free to deliver any training they see fit; teachers have little control over their access or direction of training. Most teacher training is experienced during the initial two years of a teacher's career, in one enormous indigestible package. The absence of a transparent entitlement to career development has left teaching far behind other professions, which often have clear and defined routes to advancement, mastery and rank. It also denies teachers the ability to drive their own development in their own direction, and remedy their own deficiencies or develop their strengths.

In short, the contemporary teacher has little liberty to act in any way contrary to their training, management or incentives. Teachers are reduced to being delivery mechanisms; vehicles for an approved form of education. They are postmen.

## Emerging solutions: new movements in teaching

There may be some hope for renewal within the teaching profession. Interestingly, these possibilities have not been passed down through the traditional agencies of authority – the DfE, LEAs, unions, subject associations and teacher training institutions. Instead, they have come from within the rank and file of the profession. Emerging teacher movements that utilise grass-roots, teacher-led strategies have become more and more common. In such movements, teachers collaborate to drive their own development by sharing what they already know, or using their collective efforts to obtain more efficiently what they need. Two such movements are Teach Meets, and the researchED movement.

## Teach Meets

Started in 2006, Teach Meets are free, informal meetings where teachers can share good practice, innovations, and personal insights into their work. Often organised online, these events are now a common sight on the educational calendar in many countries. Due to its flexibility, its volunteer strategy, its simplicity and its appeal to community altruism, such events appeal to many. The short sessions encourage brevity, impact, and usefulness.

TeachMeets are now regular occurrences in Scotland, England, Northern Ireland, Australia, Canada, Croatia, Czech Republic, Denmark, Ireland, Sweden, the USA, and New Zealand. In New Zealand the Teachmeet is virtual and is run entirely via Google+ Hangout. Worthy of remark is the entirely autonomous nature of this organisation (if it can be called that). With no central command, and no licensing body franchising out the idea, all that exists is the idea, and people willing to share it.

There are many flaws in the model, of course: without a quality filter, some have criticised the standards of some presentations. Dogmas can be replicated and repeated as easily as innovations or sound wisdom. But this is a necessary part of a process that is by its nature inclusive and altruistic. At its best, such events can be powerful crucibles of reinvention, discussion and debate. Bad ideas, exposed to light and scrutiny, can at least be dissected and called to account.

## researchED

In 2013, I started researchED. It was originally meant to be a one-off conference aimed at teachers, and focused on useful educational research. However, it has grown quickly to become an international teacher movement.

The problems that inspired its inception were many: the relationship between the practice of teaching and the research communities is dysfunctional; few teachers engage with more research beyond their initial training, and rarely beyond that. Thus, teachers, lacking familiarity or exposure to research methodology or content, have little ability to discern what policy or intervention is evidenced substantively or not. In this context, it is possible for schools to impose almost any initiative upon their staff whilst claiming that 'the evidence' justifies their decision.

The ITT most teachers receive rarely prepares them for this ecosystem, and they become helpless recipients of faulty practices. The solution to this was to bring together all communities affected by research into face-to-face situations where they can discuss, challenge and learn from each other.

In this environment, teacher voice was intrinsic to the whole enterprise. Teachers, as recipients and end users of educational research, have every right to value and discuss their experiences of research, even if that contests what academic communities are telling them. Policy-makers were welcome to these events, as important mechanisms of research implementation. Media partners were invited to discuss how they report research. Academics and researchers were brought in to explain, face and respond to the questions, challenges and approaches from their natural (but often underrepresented) partners: teachers.

The conferences have proven to be hugely successful, attracting sell-out audiences and speakers of international reputation. The 2014 conference had nearly 1000 attendees throughout the day, with hundreds on the waiting list. Part of the popularity has been down to the blend of speakers from every point of the educational map, the low ticket prices, and the community spirit that it embodies. Speakers aren't paid, most of the work is done by volunteers, and host venues are encouraged to give as freely of their facilities as they can.

It has led to a series of regional conferences around the UK, and international conferences with launches in Sydney Australia, and New York, USA in 2015. There has also been a series of smaller conferences aimed at Research Leads – an exciting new movement in UK education. At the 2013 conference I was asked how schools could meaningfully engage with research; it was suggested that they should hire an individual to act as the research champion, to be the portal for good research access. By 2014, many schools had done so, or people had self-appointed. They wanted to know how to do their new roles, so we organised an invite-only meeting at our national conference, aimed at networking and discussion of the emergent role. It led to the demand for all day conferences where the research leads, guided by their own ideas and experience, and by leading keynote speakers from the research communities, could work out for themselves what would work for them.

That catchphrase – 'working out what works' – is central to the researchED movement. It means teachers and schools deciding for themselves what strategies to employ in their schools. It doesn't rely on any outside agency apart from the will of the teaching communities to understand what they need to develop the practice of teaching. It embodies scientific technique, but also appreciates the limits of scientific methodology in what is often a craft-based enterprise. It doesn't seek to make teaching a research-based activity, but a research *augmented* one. It aims to make teachers research literate so that they are as sceptical and as critical as they are embracing and adoptive.

In essence, it asks them to take control of their own profession. It has the potential to transform how teachers view their own development, and their own sense of professional identity.

## The College of Teaching

Still a speculative entity, this professional body acting on behalf of teachers has been seen by some as a possible mechanism by which teaching could resolve some of the issues of powerlessness and lack of agency discussed above. It recently received an enormous boost when the incumbent UK government pledged £4 million to its creation and maintenance. In theory, it could regulate continuing professional development, certify teachers and provide a coherent, professional voice for a profession that lacks one.

However, two things create suspicion that this role might not be as teacher-led as hoped. Membership is envisaged as being voluntary, and there is little sign of enthusiasm for the project outside of a small group of early adopters. Indeed, it is difficult to gauge how many teachers outside of the small, vocal online community have even heard of the proposal.

Secondly it has been decided to open membership to the college to 'anyone with an interest in education' – a definition so broad as to be open to almost anyone. Many have pointed out that if the College of Teaching isn't to be reserved for teachers, specifically those working within schools, then it cannot be said to represent a coherent community. Without wishing to convey unnecessary pessimism, the view that this could easily become the General Teaching Council Mk 2 is not unwarranted.

## Other green shoots

Other structural reform in the last five years has contributed to – in theory – the rise of teacher autonomy. For example, the conscious effort of the recent regime to harrow the vast and confusing amount of DfE guidance that served no purpose other than to evidence administrative effort. The accumulation of more and more non-statutory advice is the natural reflex of the bureaucrat, but a dead weight on the hand of a professional.

Another important reform was the decision to discontinue the use of levels as the key metric of pre-KS4 attainment and progress in 2013. Designed to be a portable indicator that could be used to compare any child in any school with any other child and school, from the beginning they suffered from many weaknesses: if Ofsted grades were often fictions with enormous variations, pupil levels were akin to pinning a tail on a donkey. With the removal of levels and the concomitant opportunity for schools to devise their own systems of assessment, notionally at least an enormous power has been devolved (or perhaps revolved) to the teaching profession.

However, most schools are, at the time of writing, still using levels. Part of the problem is that the teaching ecosystem has been deskilled; few teachers are confident enough to grapple the issues surrounding assessment due to the paternalistic relationship enjoyed with the National Curriculum and exam boards. Further, the Ofsted inspection insistence that schools demonstrate – by any means they please – progress and attainment, means that schools have to be sure their internal systems are as ostensibly robust as levels were (or were believed to be). That climate of uncertainty understandably leads many schools to stick with the devil they know.

At a structural level, Gove's free school and academy reforms were aimed at the removal of schools from LEA control. Controversial as these may be within the teaching profession, they undeniably hold enormous opportunity for autonomy. Too much autonomy, for some. Patterns within the profession are variegated; some teachers believe that independence and agency are over rated values in education at specific levels (usually structural); that schools need to act collaboratively in order to benefit from economies of scale and hive skill bases. Others believe, as I do, that such economies can be obtained from chains and clusters as well as regional, geo-political entities, and that the benefits of liberty, however terrifying, are necessary components of the revitalisation of the teaching profession.

In fairness to the organisation, some progress has been made within Ofsted. Internal reformers such as Michael Wilshaw, Mike Cladingbowl and Sean Harford have listened to the main concerns of opponents, even to the point of openly debating the issues with teachers at conferences and through social media. Inspectors have been clearly directed to ignore teaching styles, and it has been made explicit that lessons are now not graded individually. Time will tell if these gear changes are superficial or lead to genuine change. The fear of Ofsted leads many schools to anticipate their focuses, and many schools are still reluctant to let go of their protective charms, however spurious and ineffective they may be.

In summary, the present picture of teacher professionalism and autonomy is grim; it is a profession harrowed of agency. However, some green shoots of hope can be seen. It is not inconceivable that the profession could revitalise and reinvigorate itself from within, from the ground up, rather than wait for someone else to step in, *Deus Ex Machina*, to remedy its pathology. Indeed, it could be said that this passive attitude, slowly hewn over decades, could be the reason why teacher autonomy was so stripped in the first place. Time will tell. Teachers have the capacity to grasp their own futures, to design them, to become architects of their own status- as long as they remember why they are important in the first place.

### Endnotes

1  Blake, J. D. 'What should the political parties promise on education in 2015', speech at Policy Exchange Education Conference, 7 June 2014.

2  Burns, J. 'New training plan risks teacher shortage, study warns', BBC, 2 July 2013.

3  Ibid.

4  Department for Education, 'New school-led teacher training programme announced', 14 June 2012.

5  Carter, A. (2015), 'Carter review of initial teacher training', Department for Education, p18

6  http://samfreedman1.blogspot.co.uk/2015/04/the-birth-of-zombie-statistic.html [accessed April 2015].

7  Stewart, W. 'There is no right way to teach, says Ofsted inspector in exclusive TES interview', TES, 13 September 2013.

# Charter schools:
# Lessons from America's experiment with autonomy and accountability

## Doug Lemov and Joaquin Hernandez

For the most part, schools are a 'black box', a term used by engineers and scientists to describe a situation for which there is no formula of inputs known to reliably produce positive results. Ideally we could just say, "Great, let's reduce class size from 28 to 25 and ratchet up our students' mathematics skills to meet the STEM challenge head on." But it turns out that tweaking inputs doesn't produce reliable or predictable results.

When faced with a black box, the best approach is to measure outcomes and allow for autonomy and flexibility on inputs. If you don't know what the right input is in terms of class size, you could make a best guess and issue a mandate to schools, or you could remain silent, hold schools accountable for academic quality (via outcomes such as GCSE scores and Ofsted inspections, as in the UK, or annual testing as in the US), and let each school decide for itself. Over time they would test ideas and get feedback, learning what works in which situations, with what caveats and synergies, and maybe even what to do when conditions change. Managing outcomes unlocks problem-solving skills among teachers and school leaders – a powerful force for good.[i]

Class size again provides an example: One school we know, accountable for outcomes, chose to have 30 children in each classroom instead of the 25 they originally planned. Adding five more children to each classroom would pay for an additional half of a teacher's salary, which was enough to hire a reading specialist for every two classrooms. She would split her time between them, pushing in during language arts blocks and reducing class size by half *at the specific time of day the school thought mattered most (literacy block)*. This is a classic 'managing outcomes' decision – it pushed the school to consider not *whether* to have small class size but *when* and *how*.

This also serves as a useful example because, despite the school's best hopes and the artful logic of the plan, it didn't work. The school just didn't see the results they hoped for. Leaders talked to teachers and they all reflected on the data together, deciding instead to invest in the teachers' assistants who were already working in elementary classrooms. They made the assistant jobs 'co-teacher' positions, increasing pay and responsibility, making the job was a training ground to become a lead teacher, and hiring young, aspiring candidates early in their careers to fill the jobs. They made

---

i   We should be clear that 1) managing outcomes requires good, rigorous and objective assessments and 2) we think the school, not the teacher, should be the unit of accountability. If schools must succeed, school leaders will take everything they know about teachers into account in assessing their work.

sure the selection process for co-teachers was just as rigorous as it was for teachers. Co-teachers weren't there merely to shuttle kids to the bathrooms and deal with strugglers; they prepared and were often called upon to teach- sometimes half the class; often a full class of students once they'd proven ready. This time around assessment scores ticked up steadily across the building, first on internal measures and then on state tests.

Thousands of schools doing this kind of problem solving, often taking different approaches and finding different solutions, is a powerful force. It means more choices to match what different families want and more knowledge generated across the system. The autonomous decisions of a diverse group of smart people, it turns out, almost always outperform the decisions of an expert. Smart systems faced with complex problems learn to decentralize problem solving, and those that do this best ultimately rise to the top.

The American charter school movement in particular was founded to tap into the power of the ideas that are generated when greater autonomy is paired with greater school-level accountability. It began in the state of Minnesota 1991 and has since spread to 43 states and more than 6400 schools enrolling over 2.5 million students.

This combination of autonomy and accountability makes charter schools a potential hot house for learning. We use the word 'potential' because 'charter schools', often referenced as if they were a consistent entity, represent a dizzying array of educational approaches in a range of regulatory environments that can be strong or weak on accountability and strong or weak on autonomy. Where the regulatory environment has struck the right balance between accountability and autonomy, in cities such as Boston and New York, the gains have been significant. A recent study by a research institute at Stanford University called CREDO, demonstrated that schools in these two cities have the strongest levels of achievement of any urban schools in the US.[1] Another study found that charter schools in New York City, on average, significantly outperformed the traditional counterparts.[2]

And if you look at a core of networks and schools that tend to approach schooling in roughly aligned ways – academic rigour, preparing children for college, clear structures – you see evidence of the potential for transformative results at scale.[ii] A 2012 study by Mathematica Policy Research and the Center for Reinventing Public Education found that students who attend schools run by high-performer Charter Management Organizations (CMOs) make learning gains of up to three years within two years of enrollment.[3] And most importantly to us, a 2013 study by found that low-income students at Uncommon Schools (where we work) performed so well in math and reading that the effects of attending 'completely cancel out the negative effect associated with being a student in poverty.'[4]

---

ii   You may associate charters with these types of structured and rigorous schools run by such non-profit operators as Uncommon Schools, KIPP and Achievement First but if you want to find the most constructivist schools in the US, they might just be charter schools too. Chartering is a regulatory strategy the promises freedom, which schools have used in a wide variety of ways.

These early returns are not a guarantee of victory. There's no parade down the high street yet, just early, promising evidence with many miles left to travel. But we have been insiders to this process of knowledge building. You might even say we live inside the black box: we are employees of Uncommon, and members of a team set up to study and learn from teachers and what they do to maximize achievement. Our daily work is to study what teachers do as problem solvers and to share it within Uncommon and externally. Doug's books *Teach Like a Champion* and the revised *Teach Like a Champion 2.0* have been the best-selling teaching books in the US for several years running and have been translated into eight languages.

Charter school reform, meanwhile, has grown to become highly influential and controversial, both for the schools it has given rise to and the influence they have exerted over schools in the US more broadly. Traditional school districts have sought to copy or apply many of their ideas and parents, empowered by charter schools to be able to select schools for their children for the first time, have begun to advocate for more choice and influence over what happens in their schools. In the UK, the "free schools" reform is in many ways an effort to tap the dynamism spawned by charters in the US.

With that context, here are a few of our lessons:

## Lesson #1: Be wired to learn

Successful schools must be wired to learn. Great schools are full of data, gathered to make sense of all the things that happen within their walls: Who is completing homework? Which teachers are sending students to the office? Which students? Which sorts of math problems can students not yet solve? What kinds of texts do students still struggle to read? But although being wired to learn involves gathering data, it isn't really about technology. It's first and foremost about low-tech human interactions and how you use the data. As one colleague once noted, if your data culture is right, you don't need to use anything fancier than a pencil.

The first step is establishing a Culture of Error, where staff members feel safe exposing challenges and learning from mistakes. The goal must be not so much to make the fewest errors as to learn from mistakes faster than anybody. If employees feel they must hide their struggles, schools will only find out about them after they have grown, spread and become much harder to deal with.

Doug was recently struck by the importance of this when he crossed paths with a teacher he knew in the hallway of Troy Prep Elementary in Upstate New York. The teacher was coming briskly down the hallway and he greeted her. "How are you?" he asked.

"Fine," she said, "but I can't talk right now. I just taught a really bad lesson and I've got to find Katie so we can talk about it." This was a remarkable moment. First, it was one of the best teachers in the school. Even so, her mindset was ego-less, focused on constant reflection and improvement. Second, she was actively seeking to share a perceived failure with her colleagues knowing that they would help her fix them.

But the true power of the story lies in the fact that 'Katie' was in fact the principal of the school. If there is greater evidence of a healthy culture in a school than a teacher seeking out her principal to deliberately share her struggles we do not know what it is. A leader's primary responsibility is to make her teachers better, so her teachers must not fear punishment or judgment for revealing that they struggle at one of the hardest jobs in the world. This is not to say that teachers are not accountable for results in the long run – accountable to Katie, in fact – just that a strong leader is able to distinguish the normalcy of daily failure from the urgency of long term success. The freedom to fail in the short run is implicit in the ability to succeed in the long run.

As a starting point for building Culture of Error, leaders often model for their staff what it looks like to embrace and learn from mistakes. At one school we know, the principal regularly solicits constructive feedback from her teachers during check-ins. She then acts on the feedback, often making it transparent to her staff precisely when and how she is doing so. At another school, leaders routinely share their own PD goals with their staff, or what they're actively working to get better at in their current role. Making goals public helps normalize the process of improvement while increasing leaders' accountability to achieving those goals.

## Lesson #2: Little things have big muscles

One thing we learned from reading Chip and Dan Heath's outstanding book on organizational change, *Switch*, is that we often assume that the size of a solution must match the size of a problem. In fact large problems can often be solved through relatively small solutions and this truth applies to many aspects of schools and classrooms. Take, for instance, the experience of Ben Davis, a former high school teacher in New Orleans, Louisiana. While interviewing for a teaching position at Sci Academy, a top performing charter school in New Orleans, Davis recounts how founder Ben Marcovitz visited to observe him. At the time, his classroom was in disarray and he was having difficulty getting his students to follow directions. At his lowest points, he questioned whether teaching was a good fit for him. Maybe working at Sci would be better, but maybe not. There was always the option of going to graduate school and starting a new career.

After observing Davis's lesson, Marcovitz offered some useful feedback: *narrate the positive behaviors in the room, in order to put the focus on what was going well and also provide a reminder to students who may not have internalized the instructions the first time.* At first, Davis was a little skeptical because Marcovitz's suggestion seemed too simple to address such an intractable problem. But the next day, he gave it a try, and to his surprise, it worked. Within seconds of giving a direction and narrating the positive ("I see Jonnisha beginning work immediately"), a few more students began to follow his direction, and then several more.

Davis's encounter with Marcovitz, which he now describes as a 'revelatory' moment in his life as a teacher, positively changed the trajectory of his classroom and career in education. Over time, Davis developed into a master teacher, and later rose to become principal at George Washington Carver Preparatory Academy, a Sci

Academy school. His story, while not altogether unique, illustrates how teachers often use small, humble solutions to overcome the challenges of their profession and to ultimately become the educators they aspire to be.

Top schools have come to recognize the power of a similar calculus. Even though the scope and complexity of the challenges are daunting, one of the early takeaways from school-based problem solving is that small and simple solutions can often be remarkably powerful. If school leaders or teachers greet students outside the door of the school every morning and shake hands with each child as they enter, they build relationships with students, while reminding them that expectations within the building are a little higher than elsewhere. Mornings start more orderly with this reminder. This tiny interaction at the door has effects that cascade throughout the building.

## Lesson #3: Schools are first and foremost cultures

Some schools think about behavior — often what things they don't want to allow to occur; the best schools think about culture- not so much what they *don't* want to happen as what they *do*. Behavior is unpredictable but culture should be predictable, a constant, and the most successful schools realized quickly that one of the first things they had to do was to intentionally shape, and often re-shape, student perceptions. This may include their relationship to the school; the long-term payoff of academic work; or their ability to do the work, even when it got hard, even when they had failed before, even when others told students, "don't even bother trying; you will only fail." School can be the voice that instills in students an alternative view of the world – one that values self-reflection, self-discipline, joy in work, math, Dickens, Darwin, compassion and consideration for others.

The work, in short, is not just academic. A school is first and foremost a culture. Like any culture, it has the capacity to shape the words and thoughts its members use to frame their experience; it binds people together. This perhaps is why you'll see so much chanting and singing at some charter schools – name us a culture in the world that doesn't use songs to express and reinforce its values and beliefs. This is why great schools go to so much trouble to build their own vocabulary for things – the 'XYZ academy way'– as all cultures are shaped by the language they use to describe what they hold sacred.

Most importantly, a school forms a culture whether teachers and leaders intentionally shape it or not. This to us is the most common blind spot. What happens in lieu of intentional culture is a distortion formed by neglect of intention, an accidental pastiche of whatever pop culture fragments and local street bravado find their way through the school doors. Instead of an assertive, positive school culture, the culture is formed by whatever voices win out when the loud, the self-indulgent, the stoic, the caring, the thoughtful, the asinine and the absurd are jammed into the cafeteria with no organizing principle.

Top schools start with a vision of what culture should look like if things go right.

Well before "grit" was common parlance, successful charters began by framing the virtues that they aspired to instill: perseverance, respect, compassion. Once during an interview, Doug asked a leadership candidate what goals or activities she would continue to pursue even if the data told her they were not increasing student achievement. This was a trick question: the right answer was: "Nothing. I do what works to raise achievement. This is my job." But the candidate looked Doug in the eye and said: "Building character, helping students to know right from wrong and to live by strong values. That matters even if it doesn't show up in the data. I couldn't do it any other way and look parents in the eye. Right and wrong will at some point become life and death for at least one of our kids. We owe it to parents to frame who we will help them help their kids to become." Doug looked up from his notes to meet the forceful gaze of Stacey Shells, the first principal he would ever hire.

Great schools also do not limit their definition of culture to student culture. Adult culture is deeply important and often shapes student culture – you teach more by how you behave in front of students than by what you say "Can you have great student culture but poor staff culture?" a colleague asked us recently. "Not for long," we replied. A staff culture that has become joyless, and lacking in team spirit is a leading indicator of what student culture will soon be like.

## Lesson #4: CPD embedded into the fabric of the school

In high-performing schools, teachers receive support from all angles. For instance, let's say a teacher was working on improving his radar – his ability to see the classroom – and the subtle cues he sends to students to show them that he sees and notices whether they do what he asks (in *Teach Like a Champion 2.0* we call this skill, *Be Seen Looking*). He might participate in a workshop where he would study video of other teachers and then practice using and adapting what they do. Importantly, this training session would likely include the best teachers in the school. This would help provide developing teachers with great models of effective teaching during practice and provide them with great models of professionalism.

Later, his grade level chair might sit in to observe and give him feedback. They might discuss in a one-on-one check-in. Afterward, he might be asked to try the coach's advice in his class and send a follow up note with observations about what worked and what didn't. (Asking the teacher to respond with details on what didn't work communicates that things won't go perfectly; that struggle is normal). The school, in short, would try to establish a culture of implicit accountability – where it goes without saying that the feedback you get should be used, not just listened to, and that the goal for every teacher is to get a little better every day.

Whatever form these levers of professional development take, the key idea is that professional development is embedded in the life of the school – in its systems of observation and supervision and its on-going conversations. Training also works better when it has a cohesive focus and teachers are asked to develop fewer skills better. For instance, of the best things leaders at the North Star schools in Newark NJ do is share a teachers PD goals across administrators so three people aren't asking a young teacher to work on three different things at once. When too many priorities and action steps compete for a teacher's time and attention, the result is often sub-par execution and diminished teacher morale.

## Lesson #5: Choice is powerful – and misunderstood

Choice is a powerful thing and it reinforces accountability in critical ways. Test scores and inspection reports are common indicators of school's effectiveness, but another is whether parents choose to enroll and keep their children in a school. One defense against schools achieving results by simplifying the curriculum and aiming too narrowly to master only the test (most top schools don't actually do this in our opinion) is that parents tend to object. One of the most corrosive forms of 'teaching to the test', for example, is dropping (or reducing) art and music from the school program. Fortunately, parents value those things deeply and express their concern if their kids don't get them often by voicing their thoughts or choosing another school. We do not think it is an accident that one of the things Ark schools – who run the vaunted King Solomon Academy and other high performing academies – prize most is their music program.

Just as importantly, choice creates an incentive for school diversity. Imagine a vociferous debate between two educators – let's assume they are school Heads – with very different visions of schooling: one holds a deep belief in the importance of factual knowledge and believes direct instruction is a productive tool for instilling it; the other believes that schools should teach universal thinking skills via project-based learning and minimize 'teacher talk.' Which educator is right? Whose vision should determine the approach taken in the schools we run?

The answer may be that they both are. Or that neither is. But why not allow them both to pursue their idea and let outcomes to settle the debate? Choice allows us to stop arguing and start implementing. We are pretty sure that there is no one 'right' school for all kids – many parents who have more than one child will recognize that the 'perfect' school for one of their children might be different from the 'perfect' school for another. It's better if the Heads just each go run their school instead of arguing.

Surprisingly to many, *teacher* choice is just as important. Imagine for a moment an outstanding Head teacher who has built a rigorous academic program in her school by increasing the amount and quality of student writing in her classes. She and her leadership team have implemented this across the school, meeting with teachers to build and revise their lesson plans. The program undergirds their outstanding test scores, and has built a deep and rigorous academic ethos in the school. It is something the school promises to parents and which parents value about the school.

To continue to execute they must be able to say to potential teachers: "This is how we do it. We write in every lesson. We will expect that of you every day." If the teacher says: "Well, I have been a mathematics teacher for 20 years and I think writing during class is hogwash," or "I've always thought it was too stifling for children to have to spend so much time writing. I just prefer to do something else," hiring them would undercut the school's approach. A school trying to implement a vision of schooling cannot have staff members sitting, arms crossed, in staff trainings playing the role of *refusnik*. They may be wonderful teachers but it would be a poor decision to hire them just as those teachers would be more gratified at a different school that shared their vision so it would be also a poor decision for them to accept the job. Teachers, like parents, should be able to choose a school based on its approach. This too exerts positive accountability on schools. If you cannot hire and retain teachers to execute your model, you perhaps you should question the model.

## Lesson #6: Hiring? Sure. Keeping and growing? Absolutely!

"The quality of an education system can never exceed the quality of its teachers," Sir Michael Barber has famously observed, and there's a lot of talk in the US about attracting more and better people to teaching. Certainly attracting top quality candidates is critical to the success of schools, but teacher quality – or teach*ing* quality, as we prefer – is not just about to hiring. Even more important are the tasks of keeping and developing teachers, especially the highest performers, so that those who want to commit their life to this profession are rewarded with the success they deserve.

Top networks have essentially made it their strategy to be is the best at making people better. This builds a culture of improvement, and attracts the kind of people who want to be outstanding at their work. And critically, when they get the support they need to do excellent work, teachers are more likely to stay and contribute their talents. It's a self-perpetuating cycle: invest in people and they will give you their best. Continuing to make the best people better is one of the challenges top schools are most passionate about.

Good people stay in their jobs for a variety of reasons. They stay because they believe their work matters and they make a difference. They stay because they like and respect their colleagues and have fun with them. They stay because they like and respect the person they report to. They stay because they have the tools they need to achieve success. They stay because they are recognized or thanked for their talent, commitment and skill. They stay because the workplace environment is warm, supportive and collegial and, in the case of teachers, that includes the classroom work environment.

All these things are important and all of them respond to engineering and culture. It is the sort of situation a school with a lot of experience in problem-solving relishes trying to solve. So while most top charters try hard to free-up every available dollar to pay the people who matter most – their teachers – as much as they can, they spend a lot of time engineering what you might call 'non-financial compensation' as well. Going home at the end of the day knowing you made an immense difference in children's lives and knowing that your organization is deeply aware of how valuable your work was cannot put food on the table. However, it can keep you teaching for a lot longer if it comes in addition to the compensation that does put food on the table.

## What's next?

So, those are some of our lessons. But of course if we are doing our jobs well, we are constantly tackling new challenges; embracing the places where we still struggle. As an example, one of the major challenges we are wrestling with now is reading. In math, a top charter school in the US can close the gap between children of poverty and children of privilege in just a few years. In reading progress is much slower, so closing reading gaps as quickly as possible is currently challenge number one.[iii]

In addition, top charter operators are increasingly being asked, or allowed opportunities to try, their hand outside the traditional confines of choice turning around district schools – the equivalent of a school chain sponsoring an academy conversion in the UK. Can charter operators work their magic when they keep the same kids and families have not chosen them as directly? Can they turn schools around when most teachers are inherited form the old school? Can they, in the words of Paul Bambrick, make buy-in an outcome of their management, rather than a pre-requisite? Time will tell.

Finally, can top schools sustain the initial success when they are no longer the shiny new thing? When they aren't in a state of constant growth that promises new opportunities to design and lead to almost everyone who proves ready? When they are less the exciting exception and more every day structure of schools?

These and many other questions remain to be answered. But we remain optimistic about the power of school-based problem solving and the unleashed talents of the individuals within them to tackle these and the thousand other challenges inevitable in the life of a school. Educators, it turns out, are remarkably resourceful when you let them be.

### Endnotes

1   Center for research on education outcomes (CREDO) (2015) *Urban Charter School Study Report on 41 Regions*, Stanford University.

2   Hoxby, C. M., Murarka and S., Kang, J. (2009) *How New York City's Charter Schools Affect Achievement, August 2009 Report*, Cambridge, MA, New York City Charter Schools Evaluation Project.

3   The National Study of Charter Management Organization Effectiveness (2012), *Charter-School Management Organizations: Diverse Strategies and Diverse Student Impacts*, Mathematica Policy Research.

4   Woodworth, J. L. and Raymond, M. E., (2013) *Charter School Growth and Replication*, Center for research on education outcome, CREDO, Stanford University.

iii   We hope that a tiny step forward in this process will come with the forthcoming publication of Doug's book (with Erica Woolway and Colleen Driggs) *Reading Reconsidered*.

# Postscript

## Robert Peal

Prior to his removal as Education Secretary in July 2014, Michael Gove took to teasing his more obdurate opponents by prefacing meetings with the statement, 'Now that I am approaching my halfway point as Education Secretary...' There is little doubt Gove would loved to have reprised the role in the new Parliament. Instead it falls to Nicky Morgan to bed in the last five years of education reforms.

As this collection of essays demonstrates, the previous government bought about revolutionary changes to school structures, qualifications, and teacher training. For the next five years, the major concern must be entrenching existing reforms, and allowing them to become stable fixtures within England's education system.

A less pugnacious and single-minded figure than Gove could never have achieved such radical change in such a short space of time. However, as is so often the case, his attributes may also have been his undoing. I have often heard Gove supporters concede that he did not carry enough of the teaching profession with him in support of his reforms. Though it made for enlivening debates, bellicose rhetoric in the *Daily Mail* attacking 'enemies of promise' and 'Marxist teachers' was quickly construed as teacher bashing.

For this reason, the more emollient figure of Nicky Morgan, who promised the profession 'stability' whilst on the campaign trail, could be the right person to see through the next stage of school reform. The best-case scenario is that she will continue the spirit of Gove's reforms, but allow for some healing to occur between the profession and the government. Morgan should be aided by the fact that, though Gove may be gone, many of his appointees remain. At Ofqual, the National College for Teaching and Leadership, and the Department for Education, kindred spirits in the crusade for higher standards and school autonomy remain firmly in place.

The worst-case scenario for Nicky Morgan would be a rerun of the last three years of John Major's government. After a period of energetic reform during the early 1990s, Gillian Shephard (a former teacher) was made Education Secretary with a similar mission to heal wounds. Education was kicked into the long grass as a political issue, reform went cold, schools experienced three years of benign neglect from Westminster, and in 1997 John Major ran for re-election on the rather desperate promise of 'a grammar school in every town'.

However, I am confident such deceleration will not happen this time round. Quite simply, the previous government's education reforms are too far reaching to peter out. By way of comparison, when Kenneth Baker attempted a similar policy to free schools during the late Eighties with his City Technology Colleges, he founded 15 such schools. The coalition government founded 253 free schools, and there are 500 more on the horizon.

Having been such an innovative area of coalition government policy, free schools were notable in their absence from the election campaign. This was due in part to some well-publicised early controversies ranging from Islamic extremism in one free school, to financial irregularities in another, which rather poisoned the policy in the eyes of the electorate. This time around, the DfE selection process is stronger, and there is a far increased body of expertise on hand to help out with the thorny practicalities of setting up a new school.

With a mini-baby boom currently underway, a major challenge for this government will be establishing new school places. It has been estimated that 500,000 new places will be needed over the next five years to cope with demographic growth, and an additional 25,000 teachers. There is little reason why free schools cannot plug much of the gap, though the government will be faced with the administrative challenge of planning for increased school provision within what is essentially becoming, as James O'Shaughnessy writes in his chapter, a public sector market.

The great unfinished task of the previous government is qualification reform, with the new maths and English GCSEs being taught for the first time from September 2015, and the rest of the Ebacc subjects following in 2016. They will only be examined for the first time in 2018. Morgan will have to stand firm to ensure that there is no backsliding from the exam boards away from the high academic standards set by the previous government, and will have to resist the inevitable clamour to return to modularisation and controlled assessment.

One eye-catching policy included in the 2015 Conservative manifesto was the proposal to make pupils who do not reach a level 4 in English or maths at the end of primary school retake the test after one year at secondary school. Such a policy will rightly encourage secondary schools to provide those pupils who leave primary school still struggling with literacy and numeracy with effective remedial teaching. This will give such pupils a crucial second chance to become functionally numerate and literate, an absolute precondition to accessing the secondary school curriculum ahead of them.

In a previous age of education reform, a drive on literacy would have meant central guidance in the form of national strategies, 'literacy hours' and government sanctioned literacy programmes. But not today. In recent years, the teaching of initial reading has seen a profusion of grassroots solutions where classroom teachers have developed and marketed popular new schemes such as Jolly Phonics, Read Write Inc, and Butterfuly Phonics. For schools looking to meet the new challenges posed by the phonics test and more demanding key stage 2 stats, there is no shortage of proven means to do so.

As such, recent improvements in the teaching of initial reading provide a model of what a self-improving schools system could look like: teachers and schools providing successful solutions which then spread through the education sector.

Often, when the previous government stated its belief in school autonomy, the teaching profession shook its collective head in disbelief. Freedom from local control, it was commonly suspected, was just a fig leaf for greater centralisation in Whitehall. However, as many of these chapters hopefully show, school autonomy is real and here to stay.

Unfortunately, as Jonathan Simons writes in his chapter, new freedoms are in danger of running aground upon the 'learned helplessness' of the teaching profession. This was in evidence last year, when from September 2014 schools were no longer required to assess pupil work according to National Curriculum levels. However, many Heads chose to continue using levels. The Head of one comprehensive in the South East who I talked to at the time compared such colleagues to the canary that flutters and tweets whilst in its cage, but refuses to fly out when the door is opened.

Responsibility for this fear of diverging from years of centrally mandated practice must be laid, in part, at the door of the schools inspectors Ofsted. Education has developed its own version of Godwin's Law: as any discussion concerning school improvement goes on, the probability that it will end with clamours to reform Ofsted approaches one.

School leaders are correct to say that their autonomy will always be circumscribed so long as Ofsted has the power to stamp a school as 'requires improvement' through a judgement process which has repeatedly been shown to be wanting. It is delightful for Katharine Birbalsingh to write in her chapter that she would not compromise her beliefs for the sake of an Ofsted 'outstanding' stamp, but such strong-mindedness is rare.

However, some change is afoot. In a July 2014 letter to schools, Sir Michael Wilshaw promised 'fundamental changes' to Ofsted to take effect from September 2015. These included the revision of the section 5 school inspection framework, and the introduction of 'light touch' inspections for successful schools.

Top of Morgan's agenda must therefore be to ensure that these reforms genuinely rein in the Ofsted leviathan. This could mean scrapping the Quality of Teaching grade; replacing the 1-4 categorisation scale with a pass/fail threshold; and putting an end to Ofsted's superfluous 'research and analysis' publications. A smaller, streamlined inspectorate would please everyone from right-leaning think tanks to teaching unions, and be an easy first win for the new Education Secretary.

Though Gove's sometimes antagonistic rhetoric may have prevented teachers from appreciating it, he presided over an enormous reduction in the level of micro-management guidance issued to schools. I would plead that the next Education Secretary continue in this vein, resisting the temptation to embark upon eye-catching but futile initiatives. Though it may make the occasional good headline, the Department for Education is not the place to launch central drives towards healthy eating, mindfulness, character, grit or any other educational fad du jour.

The concern that Morgan has already shown for teacher workload issue is commendable, but she must remember the most an Education Secretary can do to address the teacher workload challenge is as little as possible. Large-scale reforms to school structures and examination are necessary and underway, but government activity aimed at the everyday activities of individual classroom teachers must be avoided.

Political reforms can make school improvement possible, but it will always be individual schools and teachers who make it actual. Thanks to recent government reforms, schools now have unprecedented freedom to train their own staff; pay their staff as they see fit; create their own assessment systems; design their own curricula; take over neighbouring schools; and establish new schools from scratch. Over the next few years, it falls to schools to vindicate the belief that it is schools, not politicians, where the power to improve a nation's education ultimately lies.